Lily, A Modern Day Healer

By

Janet Jordan Fitzgerald

A special thank you to author, Shirley A. Roe for the prologue and also for all of her help and support in taking my idea for a book and helping me to bring it all the way to publication.

ISBN-13: 978-1979333054

ISBN-10: 197933305X

First Edition 2017

Disclaimer: All characters and their situation are purely fictitious. Any similarity to any person alive or dead is purely coincidental.

Prologue

By Shirley A. Roe, author

(Shirley A Roe is an award winning Canadian author of ten historical and modern fiction novels published in both ebook and print. Shirley was the managing editor of Allbooks Review International which she founded in 2000. She recently retired and spends her time travelling and looking for new book ideas. All books are available on Amazon.com. See link below.)

Janet V. Fitzgerald is a medium, healer, empath and life coach. Ms. Fitzgerald sees everyone's soul. No matter where or when she encounters people, she accepts them as whole and brimming with potential. She works with spirit, does body work, readings and gives much needed support. Much of what has happened in her own life has prepared her for this work. It has given her the empathy and understanding to see other's problems clearly. She believes everyone can heal, but first they have to ask. This is the hardest step to recovery.

After many years of practice, she wanted to share some of her case files with readers. The case files have been modified and used as part of the client's stories of the fictitious character, Lily. The problems and difficulties shared by Lily's clients are universal. It is Ms. Fitzgerald's hope that by sharing these stories, others will also be helped. The first section of this book is fictitious, loosely based on the true stories she has experienced but providing a wonderful story that readers can learn from.

The second section is actual advice and tutorials by Ms. Fitzgerald. The purpose of the book is too enlighten, educate and assist all readers to realize they are not alone. We are all united, one together in the Universe.

It is the hope of the author that you will not only enjoy reading about Lily, but also learn some valuable lessons. Thank you for taking the time to read this book.

Be sure to follow Janet V. Fitzgerald on You tube, on Facebook, and you can contact her through the following links.

https://www.youtube.com/playlist?list=PLj5jTtune4ub8AIPE4kvzuB7ou2SjvpNN

https://www.facebook.com/JanetFitzgeraldIntuitive/

Shirley A. Roe's books can be found on Amazon

https://www.amazon.com/Shirley-A.-Roe/e/B004UQ83OK/ref=dp_byline_cont_ebooks_1

Chapter One

Lily Baxter stood at the bottom of the stairs. Her hands were shaking. Taking a deep breath, she gave herself a shake, trying to calm her nerves. She knew she was being silly, but this was a big moment for her.

Slowly she ascended the narrow staircase leading to the second floor. Eyes down, she drew a deep breath when reaching the top and the small hallway. Slowly she raised her head, letting her eyes focus on the door at the end of the hall. There it was, her office!

Although Lily could help her clients wherever she was, opening her own office gave validation to her profession somehow. She had waited a long time to feel she had finally arrived. Her mother would never believe it of the daughter she belittled and called 'stupid.'

Don't think about her, this is your moment! The voice in her head was right, she would focus on her success and enjoy this present moment.

Standing in front of the door, she let her fingers brush the surface of the sign. Lily remembered the pimply faced boy at the sign shop and his frustration when she couldn't decide what she wanted on the sign. She could still see him as he drummed his fingers on the counter, waiting impatiently. And when she finally made her decision, he gave her a look of astonishment.

Her fingers rested on her name. 'Lily Baxter.' Directly beneath were the words, 'Everyone Welcome.' Lily did not like labels. Labels separated people in Lily's mind, and she was all about oneness. The pimply boy wanted her to add a line telling people her profession, but Lily knew that her clients didn't need labels. She was happy with the sign.

She flipped her blonde, shoulder length hair off her face, smoothing it in place. This was the big moment. Her best friend, Nicole had taken charge and set the office up for Lily. This was the first time Lily had seen Nicole's handiwork, but she trusted her friend explicitly.

Opening the door slowly, she stepped into the room. She let her eyes wander. The two tall windows allowed the bright sunshine to flood the room. Sheer white curtains were draped back to allow the light in. Her desk sat kitty corner at the back of the room and a large leather chair sat behind it. To the left was the place where all the work would be done. Two large throne chairs in a deep green, faced each other. A small table sat between them, decorated with a bowl of Gardenias floating in water.

The walls were painted a pale beige. She paused for a moment on the walls. Not sure if she liked the color, Lily considered changing it once she got settled. Everything else was wonderful. Her favorite pictures of Italy graced the wall behind the chairs. The Colosseum, the Leaning Tower of Pisa and the Ponte Vecchio stared back at her. *One day, I will see you in person*, she thought. Standing tall and confident, she announced, "My office!" Lily was pleased.

"Hello, can I come in?" Nicole appeared in the doorway. Lily spun around to face her friend. "Did I do a good job?"

"You are wonderful." Lily ran and put her arms around Nicole. "I absolutely love it!"

"Even the beige walls?" Nicole knew her so well.

"I can change them later." Lily laughed, hugging her friend tightly. "Nicole, I can't thank you enough. I was so excited when you told me this office above your shop was vacant, but I never imagined you could turn it into my very own happy place. It is perfect. I can't wait for my first client. Thank you so much!"

"You are welcome. Now let me look at you. I see you chose professional over Bohemian today. Good choice." Nicole adjusted the collar on Lily's grey blazer. The matching skirt and white silk blouse made her look very businesslike. With a friend like Lily, Nicole never knew whether she would show up in a flowing gypsy skirt and long beads or a business suit. That was one of the things she loved most about her friend.

"Okay, I am satisfied that my new tenant will pay the rent on time and is happy with the décor. Get ready for your first client. You are in business!" With that Nicole turned and disappeared into the hallway leaving Lily smiling widely. How she loved that woman!

Nicole owned the Gastown Bookstore on the main floor of the building. She called Lily immediately when her upstairs tenant gave notice. Lily hesitated at first, but after discussing it with Keith, soon realized that she should take advantage of this opportunity. With Nicole's help, here she was. Lily remembered how she and Nicole met at a book signing in the bookshop only three years ago. It seemed like a lifetime. What would she do without her best friend?

Giving her head a little shake, she realized that it was ten o'clock and her very first client in her new office would be arriving soon. Lily walked over to her desk, slid the leather chair back and slowly sank into the soft pliable leather. Opening the side drawer, she removed the appointment book and opened it on the desk. The first entry read, Colleen Johnston, ten o'clock.

"Ring, ring." Her cell phone rang startling her.

"Hello." Lily picked up the phone.

"Hi Honey, just checking in to see how you and your new office are." Keith was worried that Lily would lose confidence once she walked through the office door.

"My new wonderful, magnificent office and I are just fine. Thank you for calling Keith, my first client will be here any minute."

"Okay talk later." He understood that she wanted to be ready.

"Love you, tell you all about it over dinner." Lily tidied the desk as she talked.

"See you tonight, love you too. Good luck today." The phone went silent. Lily smiled fondly. Keith was a wonderful husband and father and Lily loved him very much.

The first client of the day was a young woman in her 20s. She arrived a few minutes after ten, looking very nervous. "Hello, am I in the right place?"

Lily looked up from her desk as the petite woman entered the room. "Good morning Ms. Johnston. Yes, I am Lily Baxter."

"Please, call me Colleen." The woman was wearing a raincoat, which she quickly removed.

"Nice to meet you Colleen. You can hang your coat over there. Have you had any previous or similar healing work?"

She appeared nervous, her eyes moved rapidly around the room. "No but I am aware of this kind of work…."

In an effort to calm her, Lily motioned for her to sit down. "That's good. I can explain how I work. Would you like some herbal tea?" The young woman nodded in the affirmative, her eyes still wondering around the room nervously. Lily walked to the sideboard and prepared the tea. A large wooden box filled with various herbal teas sat to the left of the tea service. Lily lifted the lid, all the while chatting about the Vancouver weather to help put Colleen at ease. She decided on Valerian Root tea to help calm her anxiety.

Setting the steaming liquid down on the table between the two chairs, Lily sat opposite Colleen. "Now tell me how I can help you."

Colleen hesitated, chewing her fingernail nervously. "Well I have been diagnosed as bi polar…I have nightmares, very vivid dreams, during the daytime I feel foggy, depressed." Her speech accelerated. "I'm an artist, so sometimes I go into my room and don't come out for hours, just allowing myself to be lost in my painting…. I never feel like myself, or very rarely…." Colleen continues to describe her symptoms. Lily simply listens, sipping her own cup of tea.

"Ok…. First thing I see is that you are, more than likely, not bipolar, but I am not going to tell you to come off medication. That is for you and your doctor to decide." Lily sets her cup down. "I will say that you are like me, you see, feel and hear other's energy. You just have not learned how to control it or even know this is what is happening to you. I can assist you with what you need to know." Lily pauses giving her time to absorb what she is saying. Her face seems to brighten. "You are an intuitive empath which makes for a difficult life. I know exactly how this feels." A small chuckle escapes Lily's lips, letting her know she understands. "You feel everything and you are not aware that it is not you, but someone outside of you." Colleen nods her head, trying to absorb what Lily is telling her. "Now it's time to learn how to become aware and free yourself of these feelings you are having. This will make you more in control."

Colleen's hand shook as she raised the steaming cup to her mouth. Lily knew she had to ask her some questions that might make her anxious. She gives her a few minutes to drink her tea and relax.

"Now I am going to ask you a series of questions. I want you to take a deep breath and answer with the first thing that comes into your mind. Don't complicate it, just answer. This will help us to get to the bottom of the situation." Colleen nods her head, Lily can see she is slowly calming down.

"Have you ever gone to someone's house and felt odd? Did you go home that night or the next day feeling off?"

"Yes!" She replied with surprise. "I went to a friend's house and for two weeks I felt weird, and had nightmares."

Lily could see she was more attentive. The words were striking a nerve with her. "Okay, I want you to sit quietly for a minute. When we think back on a time, a memory, we can usually see more than we did in that moment. Our minds see everything but we only hold onto what we deem important in that moment…so go back to that night and see what else you see."

Colleen pondered for a few moments, her eyes closed. "I was fine when I got there." She hesitated for a few seconds before responding. "I was talking to this guy and something wasn't right. I could feel a strange feeling, like energy, between us. I ignored it at the time, but there was definitely something."

"Yes, in that moment you picked up something that he was feeling. When we talk with someone, we are also connecting energetically. Do you understand?"

"Yes." She sat up straighter in her chair. Lily could see the veil of confusion lifting.

"When we do this, make this connection of energy, we usually don't notice. Most people think they are just off, but energies, or spirits, see who is open or awake to this. They try to get your attention. Most have an agenda, for example, 'This is Bobby, I want to talk to him. You can do it for me.' However, you don't hear this, you just feel an energy. Do you understand?"

"Yes, I do!"

Lily continued, "Okay, now if we don't notice or become aware, spirits can stay around trying to get your attention. If we still don't become aware, we feel like we are in a fog, our eyes are blurry and we are unable to focus. We don't feel like ourselves."

"Yes! Oh, my God, that is it. That is how I feel!"

"The next step is learning how to be 'in awareness' all of the time, or at least as often as you can. You will do this so many times and it is painful. Therefore, you will want to try and stay in awareness."

"But how do I do that?" Colleen looked like someone had asked her to fly.

"Let me tell you how. When you go out, take the first few moments just to notice, be aware. Especially if you intend to drink or do any drugs, which is not a good idea as it promotes unawareness. Look and say, 'I am aware everyone has something. I am here to enjoy myself. I am not here to entertain spirits of any kind. I am not ready to do this work. I need to learn more." Lily pauses making sure Colleen is absorbing all that she is saying. "Intention, make a statement and they will respect it. Of course, there are others that won't respect it, however you will know; they are very dark and you will feel them immediately. You will know to leave, you will be aware."

Colleen looks directly at Lily. There is some confusion on her face. "How does this feel to you?"

"Okay, what if I try to do this and I forget?" Colleen asks, her tone skeptical.

"You will practice and if you forget, get back into the awareness and do it again. You are young, you will learn. If you are stuck, you reach out to me and I can clear you."

With some hesitation she replies, "Okay, great." There is not much conviction in her voice.

"You must practice. This is a gift and your gift is strong, awareness is everything for you."

"Okay." She looks down at her hands, worried that she won't be able to do it, but excited at the same time. It feels right and now she has a plan. She takes a deep breath and lets it out slowly. "Okay."

"You can do this and I am here if you need me. As you learn your way through this, you can text me if you need me but know this, you are in control. When you make a statement, it is true. You have acknowledged the energy. We must keep learning and growing. Are you okay?"

"Yes. So, I can reach out to you when I need to?"

"Most definitely, just practice this for a couple of weeks and then let me know how it is going. Remember if you need me, just reach out."

As if a great weight had been lifted, she stood up. "Thank you so much, I feel so much better. Now I have an answer and a new direction." Although she was barely five feet tall, Colleen seemed to have grown taller.

"You are welcome, remember, you are not bipolar. You are gifted." Lily put her arms around Colleen, who responded gratefully.

"I have a brochure that you will find interesting. It is about Empathy."

Colleen reached for the brochure and glanced at the first few sentences. *Empathy is the capacity to understand or feel what another person is experiencing from within the other person's frame of reference, i.e., the capacity to place oneself in another's position. Empathy is seeing with the eyes of another, listening with the ears of another and feeling with the heart of another. There are many definitions for empathy which encompass a broad range of emotional states. Types of empathy include cognitive empathy, emotional empathy, and somatic empathy.*

"Thank you, Lily. I will make an appointment for three weeks from now and let you know how I make out." Colleen picked her coat off the rack and handed Lily a check as payment. Lily wrote Colleen's name in the appointment book and walked her to the door. A feeling of great satisfaction passed over her. This was her purpose, this was why she was on this earth, to help heal as many people as possible.

On her way down the stairs, Colleen shouted over her shoulder, "I like your sign."

Chapter Two

      Lily turned off the lights and closed the door to her office. It had been a wonderful first day. At the bottom of the stairs she stepped out into the street, turned left and entered the bookshop. The shop was filled to overflowing with books. Shelves reached to the ceiling and along all three walls. A small counter sat to the right. On the corner sat an essential oil diffuser scenting the air with calming Rosemary. Several Himalayan Salt lamps glowed a soft orange around the perimeter of the room. There were big comfortable chairs scattered haphazardly giving the shop a welcoming, homey appearance. Nicole was seated at the far table with two young students. Her head was down and her dark hair hung loosely. Realizing Nicole was busy tutoring, Lily gave a little wave and turned to leave.

      "Lily! Wait just a minute." Nicole gave some quick instructions to the two wide eyed boys and walked over to Lily. "How was your first day in the new office?"

      "I still can't believe it. I had three clients today and it felt so good to be in such a safe and comfortable place. Thank you again, Nicole."

      "I love seeing that light in your eyes. Do you have appointments tomorrow?"

      "Not until eleven. I am going to take Celeste to the dentist and then drop her off at school. I should be done by ten. How about a quick coffee before I start?"

      "Sounds perfect. I'll see you tomorrow."

      "Oh, by the way, I gave out one of the brochures today. It was a great idea, I don't know what I would do without you. You are so organized."

      "Happy to be of service. Now I had better get back to those two hellions before they get into mischief. Bye Lily." Nicole waved as Lily stepped into the street.

      "Bye Nicole." She waved and started out down Water Street towards home. The rain had stopped and the sky was scattered with white puffy clouds. The sun reflected off the wet pavement making it shimmer with light. Lily took a deep breath. Life was good, she felt confident and optimistic.

Gastown was a quaint suburb of Vancouver. Lily loved the small boutiques, the coffee shops and the lovely waterfront area. Lily's office was located near Maple Tree Square on the east side of town. She strolled passed the shops, professional offices, art galleries and restaurants toward Cordova Street where she lived. The Steam Clock glistened in the sun. Raindrops dripping from its four clock faces. The clock was a popular tourist attraction in Gastown and Lily could see about a dozen people posing and taking pictures at the base of the lovely clock. Just as she drew near, the chimes began to signal the time of day. Steam operated the whistles, which produce the chiming sound, making the clock incredibly unique. Lily remembered Keith telling her that the clock was featured on a Nickleback album cover. The chimes always made her smile.

Cordova Street ran somewhat parallel to and merged with Water Street at the west end of town. Lily passed a grove of Willow trees remembering that the street was once called Willow Street because of the grove. She walked the two blocks to her home.

Lily and her family lived in a brownstone row house in the newly regenerated section of Gastown. The buildings were historic but very modern inside. She loved her three-story home.

"Hello, anyone here?" Lily removed her shoes and her coat and walked toward the bright and sunny kitchen in the rear of the house.

"Mommy!" Five-year-old Blane appeared, throwing his little arms around her legs.

"Hello Blane, that is a nice greeting. What's up with you today?"

"I am going to be a bumblebee. Isn't that great?" He could hardly contain himself. A wide smile filled his chubby, freckled face. His brown hair fell forward covering his left eye reminding Lily of a mischievous imp from one of Celeste's books. She laughed out loud.

"A bumblebee? And why is my adorable son going to turn into a bumblebee?"

"For the play! You know the school play about nature's garden. I'm going to be the bumblebee!"

"Wonderful, congratulations. Next thing we know you will be off to Hollywood to appear on a weekly television show. Love you, my little actor." She hugged him tightly.

Blane danced around the room, a loud buzz emitting from his lips, making her laugh.

"Oh, really Blane, must you buzz in the kitchen. Why don't you just 'Buzz off'?" Celeste appeared from the dining room. She playfully swatted her hand at her brother, who disappeared into the other room. "Hi Mom."

"Hello Celeste, is your father home yet?"

"No, but he's on the way. Mrs. Carter is in the living room. Mom, I really need to get the next Harry Potter book. Do you think we can go to Nicole's shop after soccer practice?"

"I thought you just started reading Harry Potter and the Chamber of Secrets. Didn't we have a deal that you would clean your room before we got any more books?"

"I'm almost done, the one I want is Harry Potter and the Prisoner of Azkaban. Please Mom, please!" Celeste was blonde like her mother and tall for her eight years. "I'll be upstairs reading, if you want me. Don't forget, soccer at six thirty!" She disappeared leaving Lily wondering what she would make for supper. Remembering the sitter, she strolled into the living room. Mrs. Carter was watching her soap opera and didn't notice Lily.

"Mrs. Carter? Hi, you can leave now. Thank you so much for staying a few minutes late."

"No problem, Mrs. Baxter. See you tomorrow." The rotund Mrs. Carter lifted her bulky frame from the sofa and headed for the front door. "You ran out of milk." With that, she was gone. Lily picked up the empty teacup and turned the television off. Keith would be home soon and she had better start dinner.

Lily liked to serve healthy, nutritious meals to her family. She decided to check the computer for a new recipe. Zucchini Bread made with sweet potatoes! That sounded interesting.

She would ask Celeste to come down and help her bake some for dessert. "Celeste!"

Lily found the coconut flour, sweet potatoes, cinnamon and other ingredients and started to prepare the recipe. Celeste arrived minutes later. "Do you want to help me make some zucchini bread?"

"Sure." Celeste's voice reflected a lack of enthusiasm. However, she took her place beside her mother and started to stir the ingredients.

Just then Keith arrived home. "Hello! Where is everyone?"

"We are in the kitchen Dad! Making zucchini bread."

"Zucchini bread, sounds delicious. Here Celeste, I brought you a present." Keith smiled at Lily and gave her a wink. Celeste, hearing the word present, deserted Lily and ran to her father.

"What is it? It's not my birthday." Celeste tried to reach the parcel but Keith held it high and just out of reach. "Dad, come on." Laughing, he handed her the surprise which she quickly ripped open. "Oh Dad, you are the best. Harry Potter and the prisoner of Azkaban!"

Lily smiled watching the interchange between Keith and Celeste. "Keith, I told her she had to clean her room before she could have that book. Celeste put the book down on the counter and if you want it, go and clean your room first."

"But Mom!"

"Celeste, do as your mother says. The book will be here when you come down." Keith looked sheepishly at Lily.

"What about making zucchini bread? Do you want me to clean my room or make bread?" Celeste replied sarcastically. Lily had given up on the idea of enjoying some quiet time with her daughter making bread and now she had to make sure she didn't give in.

"Go and clean your room while I finish this bread. We will eat and then you have soccer practice. Get going young lady!" turning to her husband, Lily continued, "And you Mister, check with me next time you bring a surprise home." She smiled and kissed his cheek.

"Duly noted, your majesty!" Keith loved to tease her. "Where is Blane?"

"Buzzing around the house practicing his bumblebee act for school. Don't tell me you brought a surprise for him too!"

"Just a new Cirque de Soleil DVD, you know he's fascinated with theater."

"Put it over there, you can watch it with him after soccer practice. You really shouldn't spoil them."

Keith reached up and dusted flour from Lily's cheek. "It is just a little treat, no harm done. Now what's for supper besides zucchini bread?" Lily smiled, she knew that Keith wanted the children to have everything in life. His own upbringing was a precarious one, being one of eight children with a single mother. She had to remember where Keith came from and not be too harsh with him. *Everyone has baggage in this life*, thought Lily. *I am so grateful that I can help people with their baggage, very grateful indeed.*

"Salmon with lemon, basmati rice and spring salad and you can start washing vegetables if you like." The phone on the wall began to ring. Keith reached for it. "Hello? Oh, Hi Conrad. How are you, buddy?" Conrad was Keith's son and Lily was expecting him to come for the weekend. "Friday night? Yes, I'll pick you up at school."

Lily prepared the bread and put it in the oven. Then she continued making the rest of the dinner while Keith chatted with Conrad. Lily loved her thirteen-year-old stepson just as much as her own two children and the five of them always had a great time together.

Later the family headed for Portside Park. Driving in from the Main Street overpass, two Chinese lion statues framed views of the peaks of the Lions; they travelled past several more beautiful and moving monuments and sculptures before arriving at the soccer field. Lily and Celeste walked over to the area where the coach and several players were waiting. Keith took Blane out to the small pier jutting into Burrard Inlet, a good place to get a close look at Vancouver's working port, with views of the colorful containers, cruise ships, heliport, and Sea buses. Blane loved looking out into the water at all the boats and small sea planes and it would keep him amused while Celeste practiced.

As they lay in bed that night, Lily told Keith about her office and what an amazing job Nicole had done. "It is just perfect, Keith. Wait until you see it."

"I'm so proud of you Lily, now you have a place to continue your work. You help so many people find their way out of the darkness and confusion. I love you, my amazing wife!"

They lay snuggled in each other's arms. Lily stroked Keith's hair, noticing a little more grey than before. He had a high- powered position and was often stressed out. She stroked his cheek. How lucky she was to have this man. Sometimes Lily wondered if she could ever help Keith find the peace that he so badly sought. She could help strangers with their problems, why couldn't she help her own husband?

Keith's mind was filled with thoughts of work. How would tomorrow's meeting go? What would happen if his boss decided to retire? Who would take over? What if he didn't like the new boss? His mind reeled as he lay awake for hours worrying. Beside him Lily slept soundly. Oh, to have her sense of peace; her trust in the Universe that things would always work out for the best. He was amazed at Lily's ability to see everyone's soul. She always saw the best in everyone, giving hope and guidance to those in need. A truly amazing woman!

Chapter Three

The next morning Lily found Nicole designing a large poster of 'Gassy Jack.' Lily admired Nicole's artistic talent. She could barely draw a straight line, but Nicole could create the most amazing works of art. "What is this?"

"Hi Lily, I am just designing the poster for the summer festival. What do you think so far?"

Lily looked at the picture of the bearded Gassy in his waistcoat and trousers and laughed. "This is our founder? Why did they call him Gassy?"

"He was called Gassy because he talked nonstop, not because he suffered with flatulence as most people assume." Nicole laughed. "Gassy Jack Deighton was a Yorkshire seaman, steamboat captain and barkeeper, who opened the first saloon here in 1867. The town prospered around the saloon with the Hastings sawmill and the seaport. Loggers, fishermen and many a sailing ship's crew spent time in Gastown."

"Didn't I read that he was married to a First Nations woman?" Lily loved Nicole's stories.

"Two actually, his second wife was Qua-Hail-Ya, but everyone called her Madeline. They had a son Richard, who died a few months after his father in 1875. Madeline died in 1949 at the age of ninety."

"Coffee?" Lily asked. Nicole nodded, putting her pastels in the case. She walked over to the small sink and washed the dust from her hands while Lily poured two steaming cups of coffee. The rich aroma of the arabica beans filled her nostrils. "New brand? This smells delightful."

"Yes, thought I would try the new organic coffee that the whole foods store is selling. I like it. Let me know what you think." Nicole plopped into one of the overstuffed chairs and pulled a footstool close to her. She lifted her feet up on the footstool, sipped her coffee and stretched her head back leisurely.

"Yum, I like this one better. What are you doing later? I thought we could go and look at the new furniture boutique that opened. I have appointments at eleven, one and two o'clock but I am free after that." Lily sat opposite Nicole and laid her own feet to rest beside her friend's.

"I can close up for an hour at three thirty. I wanted to go and look for a new table for the corner. The new computer arrives on Tuesday and I need something solid to put it on. How did Celeste make out at the dentist?"

"Moaned all the way there as usual, but the dentist said that he didn't think she needed braces. What a relief, do you know they can cost over twelve hundred dollars!"

"That's good news. Knowing Keith, he would order the very best braces for his princess and it would cost a lot more than twelve hundred. How is he? Still overworked and stressed?"

"Yes, being the CEO of such a large firm is very taxing on him. Now his boss is considering retiring and Keith is worried that he won't like the new boss, whoever that is going to be. You know Keith, worrying about what hasn't happened yet and making a mountain out of a molehill. I just wish I could find a way to give him a more peaceful approach to life." Lily sipped the hot liquid, her taste buds excited by the rich flavor. "One day I will figure it out."

"Yes, you will." Nicole patted the back of Lily's hand. "Now drink up, we both have work to do."

Lily finished her coffee and headed upstairs to her office. The sunshine filtered through the two windows, casting a heavenly glow over the room. *This is going to be a good day,* Lily thought to herself.

Lily's first appointment was a mother and her six-year-old daughter, who was having tantrums. Lily invited them to sit and needing another chair, she brought the leather desk chair from behind the desk. The little girl immediately wanted to sit in it and twirl around.

"Now can you tell me something about the tantrums?" Lily asked the woman whose name was Dorothy.

"Every day. I can't handle this anymore. I don't know what to do. I took her to my doctor and he said maybe you just need to discipline her better! I thought he was crazy and walked out on him." Dorothy was beside herself. She looked like a woman at the end of her rope and Lily knew she needed to help her find a solution. Little Abigail continued to spin herself around on the desk chair.

Looking at Abigail, Lily slowly reached over and stopped the spinning chair. "How do you feel Abigail?"

Abigail replied, "Fine. Maybe a little dizzy from spinning." She smiled.

Lily felt that perhaps Abigail felt she had disappointed her mother and would not talk in front of her. She decided to suggest that Dorothy go downstairs to the bookstore so she could speak to Abigail alone. The mother hesitantly left the room.

"So, do you know why you are here?" Lily looked at the little upturned face.

"Yes, because of my tantrums."

"Okay, can you tell me how it makes you feel when you have these?"

As the little girl spoke, Lily could feel the buildup in her stomach. Which often happens because Lily experienced what they are feeling. "Does it feel uncomfortable?"

"Yes, I don't mean to do it just happens!"

"It's okay, it does just happen, but we are going to find out why." Lily tried to reassure her. Dorothy had told her that the tantrums occurred around four or five o'clock every day. "Tell me about school, do you like it?"

"Yes I do, I really like recess."

Lily laughed, "Yes I did to, do you play with your friends?"

"Yes."

"What do you play?"

"Tag ball, it's fun!" Lily was watching Abigail closely, suddenly she pictured snacks in her mind.

"Do you take snacks for recess?"

"Yes."

"What do you usually take?"

"Chips, crackers stuff like that."

"Do you eat them?"

"Not every day."

"Do you trade your snacks?"

"Yep."

"Do you have a favorite that you trade for?"

"Yes, fruit roll ups."

"Oh, do you do this often?"

"Yes, I asked my mom to start getting them, so she did. They are fun to eat!" Now they were getting somewhere. Lily was homing in on the problem.

"I know they are." Lily felt a frustration in her stomach, confusion in her mind, she asked her, "How do you think they make you feel?"

"Good, I like them."

"What if I told you that they have some stuff in them that could be making you have those tantrums? What if I asked you not eat them anymore?"

"Why do they do that?" Abigail looked disappointed.

"There is a red dye in them. I see that is causing your problem. Your body doesn't like it so it causes you to feel bad." Lily tried to simplify the explanation so Abigail would understand. "Does your stomach feel mad or frustrated when you have these tantrums?"

"Yes, really bad. I can't get it out of me!"

"Okay Abigail, this is what we need to try to see if this is what is causing you to feel that way, because that is not you, is it?"

"No! And my Mom gets really mad. I don't want her to be mad at me." Abigail put her head down and rubbed her eyes.

"Ok, so what if we did this? I'm asking you to not eat anything that has a red dye in it. You can ask people 'does that have red dye in it? I can't eat that.' Can you do this?"

"Yes."

"You promise?"

"Yes."

"Let's try it for a week see if the tantrums stop and you feel better. Do you want to do that?" Abigail sat more upright.

"Yes, I don't like the way I feel."

"Okay, so I'm going to tell your mom not to buy you any snacks with red dye in it and at school you are not to trade for anything that has it in it. Do you understand? You can tell because it will have the color red. You can have an adult read the label if you are not sure. We are going to do this for a week and then you will come back and tell me all about it, okay?"

"Sure, okay I can do it."

"I know you can and you will feel so much better. Are you okay? Do you feel okay about this?" Lily wanted to be sure that Abigail understood. She had to remember that Abigail was only six-years-old.

"Yes, I will do it!"

"You can spin some more if you like. I will call your Mom." Lily called downstairs and asked Nicole to send Dorothy back.

"We will see you next week. If you need me call me, tell your Mom and have her call me. You are a very clever girl and I know you will do this."

"Yes, okay." Abigail began to spin, giggling as she turned around and round.

Lily explained to Dorothy that they are all going to work together and that Abigail is going to stick to it. Dorothy was a bit skeptical, but Lily knew she would. Every child wants their mom proud and loving, so Lily knew she would do it. Lily explained tantrums can be caused by many things. Most are food related. It's rarely thought out by a child. It's reactive, parents must try to be aware. Children just want parents to love them and they really do not want to act up. Food reactions are not understood by children and when they act up, they don't know why. "Seek it out, find out what is really going on with your child. There is an answer. I will see you both in a couple of weeks. Take this brochure, it will answer more of your questions."

Dorothy read the first few lines of the brochure: *Red dye allergy occurs to both adults and children, who are unable to digest red dye. Red dye is commonly referred to as food coloring #2, which is named carmine or cochineal extract. Another common source of red dye allergy is food coloring #40 which could be found in medicine and food. This ingredient is commonly used to preserve, prepare and put coloring to food. Although commonly misconstrued as food allergy, red dye allergy is actually a food intolerance.*

The increase of food with preservatives and other artificial ingredients, also paved way for the increase of people with red dye allergy. Kids are commonly affected because they fancy eating snacks and sweets more.

"Thank you so much, red dye! I never put that together. You are amazing, Lily. Abigail say goodbye to Lily." Dorothy took Abigail's hand, she looked like the weight of the world had been lifted.

"Bye Lily, thank you for letting me spin on your chair." Lily smiled at the simple innocence of children.

Lily returned the chair to the desk and sat down. She patted the pile of brochures on her desk. They were becoming a good addition to her services. Nicole had done her research well and had produced brochures and several different topics that Lily had mentioned to her. The clients seemed to like the additional technical information. *Thanks Nicole!*

After her last client of the day, Lily and Nicole walked a few blocks down Water Street to the new furniture boutique and spent an hour wandering through the shop. When Lily told Nicole about the Red Dye brochure, Nicole was surprised. "Wow, I actually thought about not including that because it didn't seem to go with all the other work you do, but something told me to print it. I guess the universe was at work, once again." The two of them laughed.

Chapter Four

Lily arrived home to find Blane crying at the bottom of the stairs. "Blane, what's wrong? What happened?" She pulled him into her arms.

"Daddy yelled at me. I didn't do anything wrong and he yelled at me. That is not nice."
Blane sobbed as Lily tried to make sense of what he was saying.

"Daddy must be having a very bad day at work and he took it out on you. You are right, that is not nice. Now you stop crying, Mommy knows you didn't do anything wrong. Wipe your eyes and go upstairs and play. I will talk to Daddy. Where is he?" Blane wiped his face and pointed to the back door.

Lily hugged him tightly and sent him upstairs, then she took a deep breath preparing herself for a faceoff with Keith. She found him sitting in the yard, head in his hands.

"Keith, what happened with Blane? Why did you yell at him?" Lily was trying to put herself in a neutral position both emotionally and mentally. She had a gift of being able to talk to her family with a detached presence that served her well.

"I shouldn't have yelled at him. He was running around making noise and I have a headache. I had the day from hell and I just couldn't cope. Tell him I'm sorry." Keith wouldn't look at her.

"No Keith, you tell him you are sorry. Look at me." Lily pulled another chair close to Keith and facing him, she took his hands in hers. "Keith, look at me."

Slowly he raised his head, she saw a deep sadness in his eyes. "Start at the beginning."

"My mother called today, right before a big sales meeting. No matter how old I am, she always makes me feel like that miserable little boy whose mother hated him." He sighed, his face filled with self-pity. "I really don't know what you see in me."

Lily took a deep breath, she went to her healing place where she could be a healer and not take anything Keith said personally. This wasn't about her.

"Keith, take a deep breath and close your eyes."

He looked at her skeptically. "Your voodoo won't help with this Lily."

She ignored his sarcasm. "Close your eyes, take a deep breath and hold it." He did it, more to humor her that anything else. "Now take another deep breath and hold it."

"I want you to tell me why your mother makes you feel that she didn't love you."

Keith gave her a look of disbelief. "No matter what I did, she was never proud of me. She always said I would turn out just like my father, and she hated him." Keith drew another long breath. Lily was pleased to see this.

"Keith, most men that have difficult relationships with their mothers, have difficulty having loving relationships with their spouses later in life. You found that out with your first marriage, but we can work through this."

The mention of his failure with his first wife made Keith shut down.

"I don't want to work through this, just leave me alone Lily! Just leave me alone!" Keith stood up and walked away. Lily sat staring at his back as he disappeared into the house. Sometimes she wondered if she would ever reach him. Why could she help other people and not be able to reach her own husband? There were times when she wondered how they had made it this far.

"Mommy!" Blane was calling her from the back door. "When's dinner, I'm hungry."

Lily smiled, Blane seemed to have recovered nicely. "I'm coming. Let's have something yummy."

When she arrived in the kitchen, Keith was nowhere to be seen. "Where is Daddy?"

"He said he was very sorry for yelling at me and then he left. I don't know where he went. Can we have spaghetti?" Celeste arrived home and Lily concentrated on making supper for her children.

Lily waited for Keith until midnight and then went to bed. He arrived home sometime during the night and fell asleep on the sofa, where she found him in the morning. Lily didn't wake him, she made coffee and went back upstairs to get ready for work.

Keith woke up a few minutes later and quickly straightened the sofa cushions. The kids didn't need to know he had slept on the couch. He realized he was still dressed. Keith poured himself a coffee just as Celeste arrived in the kitchen. "Good morning Daddy, where's Mommy?"

"Upstairs getting dressed, what have you got planned for today?" Keith sipped the steamy liquid, letting it soothe his dry throat. He felt guilty for having been so childish.

"School, then straight to soccer practice after school. I am getting a ride with Alice's parents." Turning her attention to breakfast, she slathered her toast in peanut butter and poured a large glass of milk. Blane bounced into the room.

"Good morning Blane, did you sleep well?" Keith asked hoping his son had forgiven him. Blane nodded, having put the previous day out of his mind completely.

"Daddy, can we go to the park after work? I want to try the new monkey bars."

"Sure we can, I should be home early tonight. Might even try the monkey bars myself." Blane and Celeste laughed out loud.

"What's so funny?" Lily smiled when she saw the three of them laughing together.

"Daddy, he said he was going to try the monkey bars! With his fat belly! Now that's funny." Celeste pointed to Keith's stomach. He playfully swatted her hand away.

"I don't think my belly has anything to do with it. I'll show you two." He gave Lily a weak smile. "Busy day today?"

"Four clients and then I have to help Nicole pick up a table at the new furniture boutique. I should be home for supper. You take the kids to the park and then come back and tell me all about your monkey bar experience." She tussled Blane's hair and rested her hand on Celeste's shoulder. "You two had better get to school."

When the children were gone, Keith put his hand on Lily's arm. "I am so sorry about yesterday, I shouldn't let her get to me like that. Sorry Lily. I just want life to be simple." He looked at her sheepishly.

"What you should do is try to make an effort to deal with it. The only way life is going to be simple is if you start thinking and acting differently, but I can wait until you are ready. Now off to work, we both have busy days." She kissed his cheek and he smiled. Things were calm for today but Lily knew the issues of Keith's mother would continue to raise their ugly head until Keith dealt with it properly. Why were men so hesitant to throw ego away and just let themselves be helped? Lily knew she could help Keith if he would just let her.

Lily found it strange that after the incident with Keith, her first client was a man. She didn't see many men in her line of work. She looked up from her desk, thinking that she had heard a knock on the door. She listened for it to repeat. Nothing! Lily went back to what she was doing. Again, a very quiet knock. "Come in."

The door opened slowly and a gentleman appeared. He looked anxious and unsure. "Is this the right place?"

"If you are David Duncan, yes it is!"

"I am, sorry I feel a little silly coming here today." He stepped into the office sheepishly.

Lily knew this was not going to be easy. In the back of her mind, the incident with Keith played over and over. *Men, why are they so afraid of their feelings! Focus, Lily, focus.*

"Mr. Duncan, may I call you David?" He nodded, still looking very unsure. "Please have a seat, I promise this won't hurt a bit." Lily tried to inject some humor into the situation.

"Thank you." David took the chair on the right. Holding his jacket in his hands and twisting it tighter and tighter.

"How about you begin by telling me why you wanted to see me." He hesitated but then he began to talk.

"I just never knew what it was like to feel happy, like really feel happy. I don't even know what happy feels like, or looks like. My home life was always in chaos, unhappy parents, and unhappy life."

"Do you have any idea why you might feel this way? What was your childhood like?"

"I remember watching my mother and father fighting all the time. It got to the point when it was time for him to come home, a knot would grow in my stomach. My sisters and brothers and I would go in the basement and watch TV. It was our escape. My mother started to take pain killers. It got to the point she would be passed out for days, we would have to take care of ourselves, and I was only 9 years old. My father would take us to work some days and leave us in the car all day while he worked, today that would be abuse! But it was what he thought he had to do because our mother couldn't look after us. Weird life back then for sure."

"Take a minute, while I make us some tea. Would you like green, chamomile, or basil?"

"I don't know, tea is tea to me. Whatever you have." Lily smiled and went to make the tea. She knew he needed time to relax and think about what he had just told her.

"Here you go. Please continue. How do you feel now?"

"Good, nervous, excited, hope this works or not sure what else I can do… tired of living this way."

"Okay, let's continue with your childhood." Lily sipped her tea and waited.

"Then my father left. I was almost 10. I remember looking out the window and waiting for him to come back. He never did and as many kids do, I thought I had something to do with it. So somehow, I started looking out for mom. I hated when she tried to take the pills to get numb, once I knocked them out of her hand. I didn't realize because we were all in survival mode that I was becoming an enabler. My mother was very negative, always told me who I was and who I couldn't be and what I couldn't do. I grew up fighting it. I also became a lot of who she said I would be, you see she hated men. She told us enough that we would be just like him! And though I tried not to be, I see now that there is something to the thought that someone, who is supposed to love you unconditionally, tells you over and over, that you are no good."

"How did you compensate?"

"I developed a happy, funny person outside, and a conflicted one on the inside. Later, I started reading a lot of books about happiness. I have worked through a lot of layers but the happiness thing still eludes me. What can I do? I don't like feeling this way."

"What way is that."

"Things in my life can make me sad, angry, and happy for a second but nothing I can sustain. It seems whatever others are around me feel can affect how I feel."

"Right, now let's start there. What happens when you are an enabler, especially to your mother? You develop an inner guidance compass so it will let you know what others are thinking and doing before they do it, so you can protect yourself. It's like a probe, and you need to know what going on all the time with others, like you did with your mom. Understand?"

"Yes, that makes so much sense right there I feel like something lifted." He smiled for the first time since he arrived.

"Okay, understanding this is important. You could never be happy if you depend on how others feel and how they are going to treat you. It's not a good feeling at all is it?"

"No absolutely not." He leaned forward, anxious to hear more.

"Ok, I feel we can deal with this. Are you ready?"
"Yes!"

"Okay, close your eyes. Take a deep breath, hold it, hold it, let go. Now, let's do that again. Hold, this time hold till you can't hold it any longer. Good! Okay, now one more time. Keeping your eyes closed, I am going to ask you some questions. I want you to just hear my voice. only my voice. I may touch you on the head or hands just so you know what to expect. What is it that you want to feel in your life?"

"Happy."

"Are you willing to let go of caring what others think?"

"Yes."

"Are you willing to let go caring what others do?"

"Yes."

"Are you willing to allow yourself to feel good? Do you want to be happy?"

"Yes."

"Are you willing to live your life for yourself?"

"Yes!" This answer came with more enthusiasm and Lily knew she was reaching David.

"Can you understand your mother had pain in her life to make her live this way? And can you forgive your mother for her pain?"

"Yes absolutely."

"Now, can you see yourself being happy? Are you willing to be happy?"

"Yes, yes I am!"

"Breathe." Lily touches his forehead. "You are a happy person, you are a happy person. Do you believe you can be happy?"

"Yes." David takes another deep breath.

Lily touches his hands lying in his lap and holds them, anchoring her next statement.
"Please repeat after me, I am willing to be happy. I am willing to be happy. I am willing to feel happy. I am willing to feel happy. I am happy. I am happy!" Lily let's go of his hands, her heart is open and full. David repeats what Lily has said. She continues. "David repeat, 'My heart is open and full, I am ready, I am ready. I love feeling this way, I am excited to live the rest of my life. I love my life." She stops and he repeats it over and over.

"That is very good David. Now I want you to say, "I embrace all of life and I give myself this gift. And then I want you to breathe slow and steady, feel your body, your energy, feel the lightness, the love. Feel it all David." Lily sits quietly allowing David to absorb and sit in silence for a few minutes.

"When you are ready open your eyes, look around the room." It takes about four minutes before he opens his eyes. "How do you feel good?"

"Everything looks so bright! Yes, good!"

"Can you move your hands?" David tries but he can't move. "That's okay, just sit, allow, feel." Lily noticed his face is different, lighter, his eyes are bright, filled with light. She can feel his heart filled with love. "Just breathe and experience your happiness."

After a few more minutes, Lily asks, "Can you move your hands now?" David tries and does move them slightly. "That is fine, just relax. Let it flow, let it happen."

Finally, after about eight minutes he could move his hands. Slowly he stood up, "I feel taller. How is that possible"

"It's all in how you feel about life, your life, you and who you are. Just enjoy it, don't question. Now take your time and then go do something that you enjoy. Anything, sit in nature, a park, go for a swim, take a walk, read a book. Just enjoy being alive."

He got up and smiled at Lily, "Thank you so much. I don't know why I didn't come to see you sooner." Lily went and retrieved one of her brochures.

"Here this might help. How about I see you again in a month? You can call me anytime if you need to talk."

David glanced down at the brochure before leaving. *ENABLING In the true sense of the word, to enable is to supply with the means, knowledge, or opportunity to be or do something -- to make feasible or possible. In its true form, then, Enabling behavior means something positive.*

It's our natural instinct to reach out and help someone we love when they are down or having problems. However, when we apply it to certain problems in living such as addiction, chronic financial trouble, codependency, certain forms of chronic depression -- enabling behaviors have the reverse effect of what is intended.

David left with a big smile on his face and Lily felt elated. Thank goodness, I could help him, but why can't I reach Keith? Once again, her mind returned to Keith and his problems.

On the way to the furniture store she related the past evening to Nicole. "He sounds like he is haunted by his childhood. It is too bad his mother still riles him like that."

"Keith and his siblings had a very hard life with her. She was bitter after her husband left and she took it out on the kids. Some of it wasn't her fault, she did have some serious mental health issues. To be honest, from the stories I've heard, she might have been psychic and it was interpreted as mental illness. In those days, electric shock treatment was the cure."

"Oh dear, that must have been hard. Can't you help him?" Nicole pulled over in front of the store.

"I try, but he is not ready yet. I just hope one day soon he will be, because it causes a lot of disruption in the house and to be honest, somedays I think I just can't do it anymore."

"Lily! You love Keith, I know you do. You're just frustrated." Nicole patted the back of her hand. "Now let's stop talking about this and go get my new table." Lily smiled and opened the car door. She would keep trying with Keith and hopefully he would start to see that she was right.

Lily helped Nicole set up the new table and then she walked home. She passed her favorite café where several people were enjoying the warm evening at the outdoor tables. Lily could hear snippets of conversation as she passed. "We can leave on Monday for New York."

"I think I'll order the mussels." "Of course, I don't hate your mother." That made her smile. Mothers-in-law could be quite the challenge, especially hers. If only Keith's mother would stop calling him at work. He was such a mess after talking to her and it often affected the rest of his day. Keith told her that he couldn't focus during meetings and had made a mistake on a big order after talking to his mother. She had to think of a way to reach him.

When she arrived home, the family was in the kitchen. The smell of pizza and loud laughter welcomed her. "Pizza! What a surprise." She looked over at Keith with raised eyebrows, he knew she was trying to improve their diet and junk food was off limits.

"One pizza won't hurt, and I thought I would supply supper so you didn't have to cook. Now sit down and eat." Keith poured milk for the children and red wine for he and Lily.

"You should have seen Daddy on the monkey bars, Mommy. He was hilarious."

"Well, he tried Blane. Come on, give him some credit." Celeste added with a giggle.

"Alright, maybe the monkey bars are a little beyond my present fitness level, but I am going to work on it and I'll show you two how I can swing with the best of them." Keith laughed. Lily was happy to see him joking and she had been nagging him to lose weight and start exercising for a while now. Maybe this was a breakthrough.

"Wait until I tell Conrad about today, he will think it is really funny." Blane reached for a second piece of pizza with one hand while he wiped the sauce from his lips with the other. "Conrad always says you are out of shape, Daddy!"

The rest of the evening went well and Lily didn't mention Keith's mother. He needed time and she would wait until he was ready. She did the laundry and put fresh linen on Conrad's bed, he would be coming tomorrow for the weekend and she liked to have things ready for him. Conrad was a very good musician and practiced diligently at home. Lily often wondered if they should buy a piano so that he could play when he visited. It might even be good for Celeste or Blane to take lessons. She would mention it to Keith later. Conrad's mother was a strict disciplinarian and he was a polite and well behaved young man. Lily looked forward to seeing him.

Friday afternoon, Keith picked Conrad up at school and the two chatted happily on the drive home. "Dad, do you think you could buy me a cell phone? All the kids have them."

"What does your mother think about it?" Keith was always careful not to do anything that his ex-wife Marlene, would object to. She did a fine job of raising Conrad and Keith tried to keep the peace. Their marriage had ended when Conrad was just a toddler. Keith knew it was his fault. He couldn't relate to her, he kept his feelings to himself and basically shut her out. He didn't blame her for leaving him. His thoughts turned to Lily. *I better not make the same mistake twice*, he thought. *I know Lily wants to help me, but I just don't understand all of that breathe deeply, and share your thoughts stuff.* He didn't like sharing his deep, dark secrets and talking about the past wasn't going to change it.

"Dad?"

"Oh sorry, I was thinking about something. We will talk about the cell phone after I talk to your mother." Conrad just rolled his eyes and Keith knew Marlene had already said no.

When they arrived at the house, everyone was outside. Celeste was playing her radio and singing along to the music. Lily loved having music in the house. She believed that music is good energy and it kept a good flow throughout the home. She leaned back on the lawn swing and let the music envelope her. It had been a good day so far. Blane joined Celeste in the chorus. Keith and Conrad walked into the yard. Lily smiled at them both.

"Hi, can I join in?" Conrad joined Blane and Celeste in the singing. Keith joined Lily on the big lawn swing and sat back enjoying the show.

When a Cheryl Crow song came on the three sang out loud:

"If it makes you happy, it can't be bad, if it makes you happy, then why the hell are you so sad?" Conrad stopped at the word 'hell' but Celeste and Blane just belted it out. Conrad looked at Lily and Keith, waiting for them to say something but they just laughed. Things were a lot different here than at his house. Lily and Keith didn't allow swearing in a rude way, but singing the word 'hell' in a song was not something to make an issue of. Lily could see the confusion on Conrad's face. *It must be hard with two homes, with different rules*, she thought. *I'll talk to him later, in private.*

Chapter Four

Keith drove Conrad home after a fun filled weekend. The two of them even started jogging together. It took some convincing by Conrad, but Keith finally gave in. He really needed to lose some weight and he liked spending time with his son. "Now Dad, I want you to go jogging every evening, no excuses. I will call you to remind you."

"I'll try son, sometimes after a hard day at work, I just want to sit and chill out."

"If you jog, it will help with the stress. Now stop thinking up excuses, you have to lose that gut and then you can show Blane and Celeste how you can do on those monkey bars!" Conrad laughed out loud, "That was pretty funny."

"Blane couldn't wait to tell you about that one. Here we are son, see you next weekend."
Conrad grabbed his backpack and opened the car door.

"Remember, every evening!" Keith laughed as he watched his son walk up the path towards his other home. *Jogging, who would have thought.*

Lily tidied up the kitchen. Suddenly she remembered that she was going to talk to Conrad about the cursing. She didn't want him to have difficulty with the two sets of rules and standards. Childhood was difficult enough. She remembered her own unhappy life. It seemed like a lifetime ago. Lily's parents were unhappy people. They fought most of the time. Her mother was very concerned with appearances and made sure her children dressed and spoke properly. Family problems were ignored and kept private, no one discussed their feelings.

"Mom, can we watch a movie?" Celeste interrupted Lily's thoughts.

"As soon as I finish in here. Pick one and go and get your brother. He should be upstairs." Lily pushed the past back into the recesses of her mind and concentrated on her children.

The next morning Lily arrived to see Nicole arranging a table of books outside the shop. "Sidewalk sale?" Nicole looked up and grinned.

"Why not? Whatever it takes to unload all this dead stock. I need the backroom empty."

"Why? What are you up to now?" Nicole never stopped improving her shop and nothing would surprise Lily.

"Natural Alternative therapy." Nicole announced proudly. "I have someone that wants to rent the space to do some nutritional consultation and some reflexology. Didn't you take some courses in natural therapies?" Nicole stacked more books on the table.

"I took Reiki, nutrition, and therapeutic touch. It all helps with my everyday life. It also helps with some clients. Will you advertise?" Lily helped straighten some of the books.

"He is going to put a sign out front and advertise in the papers and online. I will leave all of that to Glen."

"Glen! Woohoo, is Glen single?" Lily loved to tease Nicole about men and dating.

"Yes, he is as a matter of fact, and before you ask, he is very good looking."

"And how old is this gorgeous man?"

"Forty-one, two years younger than I am. But, this is a professional arrangement, so don't go matchmaking, Lily. Speaking of relationships, how is yours now?"

"Same as before, Keith won't talk about it and I am waiting until he wants to. We had a great weekend with Conrad. I better get to work; I have three clients today. See you later."

Lily turned left and headed for the door to her upstairs office. Nicole continued piling books on the table.

Lily's first client of the day was an unnerving one. A woman arrived, she was dark and brooding. She sat down but Lily was picking up a very negative vibration. Lily asked, "How can I help you today?"

The woman replied, "You probably can't. No one has been able to help me."
she let out an eerie laugh. "I feel I have a dark spirit around me." She paused and looked at Lily to see if she was frightened. Lily remained calm.

"Tell me more."

"It feels like a curse." The woman told Lily she married a man that was brutal to her but she couldn't leave. She now has a child and although the woman seemed concerned, she seemed more interested in making Lily uncomfortable. Lily stood up and walked to the sideboard.

"Tea?" Lily needed the break, she needed to realign to make sure she was not knocked out of her own mental and emotional place. Once the tea was ready, she came back to listen to her again. The woman went on to say she wanted revenge on her husband wanted to make him pay, can Lily do something?

Lily looked at her sternly and said, "No I cannot and will not. That is not the kind of work I do. Now if you would like to find peace and learn how to forgive or at least get to a place you can feel good about your life, I can help with that. But I do not do anything to harm another person." This was a challenging client, Lily had to stay in control of the situation.
Still bent on revenge, she sat for a while and listen to Lily but Lily knew she was just waiting for her to stop talking. The woman fidgeted in her chair. Her hands rubbed together constantly, she couldn't stay still.

Lily was right as soon as she stopped talking, the woman said, "So you won't do a curse or bad vibes or anything?" She was persistent, Lily would give her that.

"No, I'm sorry for the way your life is now but it can be so much better if you just let yourself get angry then move to the next stage."

The woman looked at Lily as if she had two heads. Lily was losing this battle. "No, I have to do something." The woman stood up and turned away.

"I am sorry but I can't help you." As they walked to the door, she turned and looked into Lily's eyes and said, "You are afraid, aren't you?"

Lily stared right back at her, "No, I am not." The woman hurried down the stairs and Lily sank into her leather chair. She opened the drawer and took out her mirror. Looking at her reflection, she wondered what the woman had seen in her eyes. She certainly hit a nerve, the woman was full of darkness. It could be scary but Lily didn't see fear on her own face and put the mirror back in the drawer. It was sad that she wouldn't let Lily help her and that she was so bent on revenge. Lily sat a moment to clear herself for the next client. She picked out a brochure and began to read:

Spirit attachment is the most common form of energetic sickness that affects more than 75% of the population in the USA? Spirit attachment is the attachment of non-physical energetic beings which attach to the human energy field (aura). These spirit attachments are human souls who have died and not crossed over to the next world. Because they did not cross over they became stuck on earth as either whole souls or parts of souls. These earthbound human souls and soul parts attach to humans to continue their life on earth, to live from the energy from humans and to maintain some type of control and power over humans. The majority of people with spirit attachments usually will never know it and will live out their entire lives with these attached entities.

Lily put the brochure down. She decided to burn some sage in her office, just to clear the air of any negativity. The smell of the smoldering sage branch filled her nostrils with an enticing and almost heavenly scent. Sage was used by many ancient civilizations to clear negativity and keep evil spirits away. She poured herself a cup of tea and waited for the next client to arrive. The rest of the day went very well.

At three o'clock, Lily was surprised to see most of the books on the table were gone. She walked into the store and found Nicole conversing with a very, good looking gentleman. "Hi."

Nicole looked over and motioned to her. "Come and meet, Glen Sloan. Glen this is Lily."

"Lily, I have heard so much about you. Would love to sit and hear all about the work that you do. I am fascinated with everything energy related." Lily stood looking into his gray blue eyes. She could feel warmth and universal love emanating from them. This was a very kind, old soul.

"Glen, nice to meet you. I am sure you and I could have some interesting conversations. I hope you do well here." She looked at Nicole, "Speaking of energy, I had an interesting client today."

The three sat down in the bookstore and Lily told Glen and Nicole about the dark woman that had come in today. They listened with fascination. "Energy has two sides, light and dark. I guess sooner or later we will encounter the dark side. Sounds like you handled it well, Lily." Glen stood and excused himself. "I have work to do. This office won't set itself up. Thank you again Nicole. The sign will be delivered tomorrow and the ad goes in Wednesday. Nice meeting you Lily, come by for a free reflexology treatment sometime." He walked away leaving the women watching him go.

"Nice, very nice." Lily poked at Nicole's shoulder.

"I told you he was good looking. It's those eyes, those very sexy eyes!" Nicole threw her head to the side with a dreamy expression. Lily laughed.

"He sure isn't wasting any time. Anyway, I better go. I must pick Celeste up for swimming and then get home for an early dinner. Blane's concert is tonight and I mustn't keep my little bumblebee waiting. Bye Nicole." Turning back, she added, "Now behave yourself!" Nicole just smiled raising one eyebrow precociously at Lily's teasing.

Lily walked to the back of the building where her car was parked. She usually walked to work, but today was a busy day and she had to get to the school for Celeste by four o'clock.

Lily sat at the pool watching her daughter swim. Celeste was a very good swimmer but that had not always been the case. Watching her reminded Lily of an incident several years before. Lily had turned her back for just a minute and Celeste had fallen into a neighbor's pool. Without thinking, Lily dove into the water. She landed on her knees at the bottom of the pool, grabbed Celeste and pulled her to the surface. Lily managed to get them both out of the pool, before she remembered that she could not swim. Lily was afraid of the water and would never trust anyone to teach her to swim. She pulled her daughter close and was filled with an overwhelming feeling of love. Parenting was a challenge Lily had never contemplated having. She really didn't think she would have children, but then and now, she was very happy that she did.

Back in the present moment, she watched Celeste taking long easy strokes. How proud she was of her daughter.

Later that night, watching Blane buzz around the stage, Lily was once again filled with an over powering love for her children. She reached over and squeezed Keith's hand. He turned and smiled, pride beaming on his face. She was very lucky to have such a wonderful family.

Just for a moment, Lily was reminded of her own childhood and how she was raised on fear. Her mother's words still echoed in her mind. *"Don't go there, you could get sick! Stay away from the pool, you could drown! You are not going downtown, you never know what could happen to you!*

"Lily?" It was Keith, the concert was over and she had been distracted by her memories.

"Sorry, I was thinking about my mother. Let's go and get our little bumblebee. He did such a good job!" Lily pushed thoughts of her mother away. *I will not impose fear on my children, their childhood will be very different from the one I had.*

When they arrived home, Keith surprised Lily by going out for a jog. "Well, you really are serious about this."

"Conrad called and reminded me, besides I have to give it a try. I really do want to lose a couple of pounds and I actually like jogging. Who would have thought it? Back soon, bye." Lily just smiled, thinking to herself, *Perhaps Keith would come around to other things that were good for him. Little by little Lily, little by little. Don't push it.*

Chapter Five

Lily could not believe that it had been two months since Glen Sloan came to work at the bookstore. "Where has the time gone?" she asked Nicole. Her friend wore a bright pink bandana over her dark hair. A pink sweater and jeans completed the outfit.

"Time flies, and now the Summer Street Festival begins tomorrow. Are your kids marching in the parade?" Nicole loaded the poster of Gassy into her trunk.

"Celeste is marching with the soccer team and Blane is dressed as a clown and marching with the school class. They are very excited." Glen appeared carrying a sign and a table.

"Do you have room for these Nicole?" She nodded and he loaded them into the car. "We have set up today and the festival starts tomorrow at eleven right after the parade. I still have lots to do." He turned to Lily, "The offer of a free reflexology treatment still stands. How about next week?"

Lily hadn't thought about it but it seemed like a good idea, "That sounds great. How about Tuesday, I don't have any clients."

"Tuesday around ten will work fine, see you then Lily. Come on Nicole, we have work to do." He rested his hand on Nicole's shoulder for just a second longer than he should. Lily picked up on the gesture, wondering if these two were getting closer. Nicole and Glen climbed into the car. Lily waved goodbye as the car pulled away.
Interesting, are you two involved?

Lily went up to her office. She didn't have clients for another hour but she wanted to take care of some paperwork. Sitting at her desk, she took out her checkbook and started to write a check to Nicole for the rent. *July 17th*, her hand froze. This was the anniversary of her father's death. It had been two years ago today that he passed away.

Lily put the pen down, her hand was shaking. Tears formed in her eyes and slowly trickled down her cheeks. *Oh Dad, I miss you so much.*

Lily's mind took her back to the past and her father's heart attack. It was a very scary time for Lily and her family but he recovered and went back to work. It was a few months later that Lily had driven him to the hospital for a follow up, when she was told the doctor was going to operate, as he needed a triple bypass. During that operation, a cancerous spot was found on his lungs. During the operation, the doctors tried to remove it. They were unsuccessful, it put too much strain on him and he passed away. She would never forget the doctor's words, "We lost him."

For more than two years Lily struggled with loss. She would see her father sitting in a chair. "Dad, you are not supposed to be here," she would say.

His ghost would reply, "I will come until you are okay Lily." As Lily sat in her office crying, she realized that she still wasn't okay. But what could she do to get over the loss of her father, the man that she went to for advice? Lily wiped her tears and blew her nose. She had to compose herself.

She decided to call David to see how he was doing. "Hello David, this is Lily. I was wondering how you are doing."

"I feel amazing. It doesn't matter what other people say or do, I still feel happy. I can be in a difficult meeting and I can just address the issues. I do not make it about me or feel I need to know what everyone in the room is going to do or think."

"That is wonderful David, I am so glad to hear that you are moving forward."

"When my wife is upset I still feel happy. I don't trip over myself trying to please her like I learned to do with my mother and therefore all women. I am happy, I never knew that happy was a feeling of just being okay with myself, that's what it is. Thank you, Lily, thank you so much."

"David, this is great. I glad to have helped you find your happiness. Take care and remember if you need me, just call." Lily hung up the phone, smiling. She was very pleased to hear that David was doing well. She thought about David's problem. This kind of work is just adjusting what the mind or subconscious repeats to us over and over. It needs to be adjusted, corrected. As children if we are told we are something or our behavior is not good, we will adjust who we are just to make sure we are loved and accepted. That's when we start splitting off, Mom loves me like this, Dad loves me like this, teacher approves of me when I act like this. When we are not loved for who we are, no matter what we do, by people who are important in our lives we must adjust. The number one fear she had found with clients is if the mom or dad can't love them, then who can? This was Keith's problem and she wished she could break through. It is hard to be a loving person if you never saw what that looks like. Lily knew that healing can help do this. It is all within. And then a strange thought popped into her head, *Physician heal thyself.* Her guides were trying to tell her something. Yes, she would have to find a way to get over her father's death.

Lily's client arrived about thirty minutes later. A woman in her fifties, smartly dressed but looking like she carried the world on her shoulders, entered the room with controlled emotions but Lily could feel that she was torn. She sat down and Lily asked, "How can I help you today, Mrs. Whitefield?"

"Well, this is difficult." The woman paused, as if trying to find the right words. "I have a daughter, Charlotte. Well, I used to have a daughter." Again, she paused struggling. "She's a boy now, Charlie, or wants to be known as a boy."

"Please continue."

"I knew she was struggling with something; she was an introvert, sad, depressed a lot of the time through her life. I didn't like the way she liked to dress, but couldn't fight it all the time. She finally came out to us. Her father is having a hard time with this. He doesn't know how to relate to her or him. She has fully changed her wardrobe and her look." Mrs. Whitefield looked at Lily as if trying to convince her. "Really if you met her you would not know she is a girl."

"So how do you feel? How are you dealing with this?"

"Okay, I guess. At first, I kept waiting for her to change back. I miss her, who she was."

"Who was she? The one you missed?"

She looked at Lily, startled by the question. "My little girl."

"If this is who your child is now, then this is who your child has been all along. The part you are hanging onto is the part that you want her to be, a conventional girl. She is showing you and has probably been trying to show you all along, that it doesn't feel right to her. Inside, she feels like a boy. Her true self is male. Therefore, who she was has always been is who she is now, she just has found the courage to share it with you and the world." Lily wanted to say the right thing, she could see the confusion on Mrs. Whitefield's face.

"I guess you are right. I'm trying. I have two girls. It's hard on everyone."

"So, let's look at this way. She is your child, her sister's sibling; she needs your love and support so she can be happy and be who she needs to be. If she was born a boy you would love her, Right?"

"Of course."

"Then this is the same. The only thing everyone is dealing with is confusion as to how to accept her change.

She could have chosen to be covered in tattoos, be a drug user, be a disrespectful kid, please stay with me here. This is just who she is, she is a boy trapped in a girl's body. And all she wants is to live her life as who she really is."

"I know." The woman looks away. A tear rolls down her cheek.

"Grieve the loss of Charlotte and accept Charlie into your life. He is your child.
How is he doing?"

"Not too good. She has a hard time with her father and sister I try to be there for her."

"Can I ask you to refer to Charlie as him?" She nods hesitantly.

"Would he come and see me? Talk with me? Let's see where he is with the change?

"I can ask him. To see if he is open to this." Lily could see the effort the woman made to refer to her child as 'him.'

"For now, just know it doesn't matter who he is, it matters how you love him. Grieve your loss; learn to love Charlie differently, until you can love him unconditionally." Now I want you to close your eyes, take a deep breath." Lily waited. "Take another, relax, take another breath. Now see yourself coming into a room, an empty room. Feel the love in the room, filled with white light. Do you feel the love?"

"Somewhat."

"Feel your breath, fill your heart up."

"Okay."

"Now I want you to see Charlotte, as she was, as you remember her to be. Let her walk in."

"Okay, I see her," she cries, tears rolling down her face.

"Go to her, hold her. Are you holding her?"

"Yes."

"Do you feel the love for her?"

"Yes."

"Hold her, just feel her, now let her pull away. As she goes you see her as she is now. Do you still feel the love for her?"

"Yes, I do."

"Pull your child in again as he is today, hold him, give him the love he needs. Put him into your heart. When you are ready open your eyes." Lily waits for at least two minutes before the woman opens her eyes.

"Hi, how do you feel?"

"I feel good. I feel like I can feel the love for Charlie now."

"Excellent! It will take time for you husband but he will come around if you do."

"I honestly don't think so but we will see. I will try and get my daughter, no, Charlie to come to see you." Lily was very pleased to hear her correct herself.

"Ask him and call and let me know if he is ready and wants to talk to someone like me."

"Thank you, thank you so much."

The two women stand and Lily puts her arms around Mrs. Whitefield and whispers in her ear, "It's all going to be okay." Lily reaches for the brochure on her desk. "Please take this brochure and let your husband read it."

Mrs. Whitefield scans the first page: *Transgender is an umbrella term for people whose gender identity vary from what is typically associated with the sex they were assigned at birth. Gender identity is someone's internal, personal sense of being a man or a woman (or as someone outside of that gender binary). For transgender people, the sex they were assigned at birth and their own internal gender identity do not match. Trying to change a person's gender identity is no more successful than trying to change a person's sexual orientation — it doesn't work. Most transgender people seek to bring their bodies more into alignment with their gender identity. People under the transgender umbrella may describe themselves using one (or more) of a wide variety of terms, including (but not limited to) transgender, transsexual, and genderqueer. Always use the descriptive term preferred by the individual. Transgender people may or may not alter their bodies hormonally and/or surgically, but it's important to know that being transgender is not dependent upon medical procedures.*

"I think this will help him. Thank you again Lily, you have really opened my eyes and my heart today." After Mrs. Whitefield leaves, Lily sits in her chair and draws a deep breath. *That was a difficult session. I think Mrs. Whitefield will be alright now. Thank you, Nicole for the wonderful brochures.*

Early morning buzzed with excitement as Lily, Keith, Conrad, Blane and Celeste headed for the festival grounds. The parade was being organized at the south end of town and all participants were to be at the meeting point at eight a.m. Long tables were spread with coffee, tea, milk, juice and breakfast delights. Celeste and Lily picked up fruit cups and bagels for the family while Keith and the boys found a table. It was a loud, crowd filled area. Colorful costumes added a festive flair to the morning and everyone was in good spirits. The sun shone brightly in a clear blue sky over Gastown.

After the parade, the family wandered through the fairgrounds. The smell of popcorn and candy floss filled the air. Squeals of laughter could be heard over the roar of the carnival rides. Lily spotted Glen's booth and wandered over to say hello. Keith waited for Blane to come off one of the rides and happened to see her talking to the handsome stranger. When Blane arrived at his side filled with excitement, Keith quickly directed him to Lily. "Mommy, that ride was a blast!"

Glen smiled down at Blane, "Who do we have here Lily?"

Lily tussled Blane's hair, "This is Blane, Blane say hello to Mr. Sloan."

"And I am Lily's husband," Keith arrived extending his hand to Glen. Lily was surprised at the boldness of the action.

"Keith, this is Glen Sloan. He is the reflexologist that I told you about, he is working at Nicole's bookstore. Glen this is my husband, Keith." Glen shook Keith's outstretched hand firmly.

"Lovely family you have Lily. Sorry but I must get back to work. See you Tuesday."

"Tuesday?" Keith looked at Lily curiously. The jealousy was something new and Lily didn't know quite what to make of it.

"Yes, he offered me a free treatment and I thought it would be interesting to learn about another alternative therapy. Now come on, we have to go and get Celeste from the ferris wheel."

Tuesday morning, Lily thought of cancelling the appointment with Glen. *This is silly, I don't need a reflexology treatment, I don't even know what it is! I'll cancel. Keith is acting strangely about the appointment and I don't need any hassles.* But for some reason, she didn't cancel and at ten o'clock she stood facing Glen in his treatment room. "Good morning Lily, have you ever had a reflexology treatment?"

"No, I have to honestly say, all I know is that is centers on the foot and energy. I am looking forward to learning something new today." Lily was nervous, she didn't know why, but she was definitely nervous. Glen explained the procedure to her, prepared the foot bath and had her sink her feet into the hot bubbly water. It felt soothing and relaxing, the scent of lavender wafted in the air. Lily leaned back and began to enjoy herself. She was glad she had chosen her knee length beige skirt and matching top so that she didn't have to roll her pant legs up.

"You soak for a few minutes and then we will begin. Reflexology is a system of massage used to relieve tension and treat illness, based on the theory that there are reflex points on the feet, hands, and head linked to every part of the body. It affects people differently. Some people get nothing from it at first but call days later to say they feel so much better. Others say it helps with aches and pains. It is a strange thing but sometimes clients actually start crying during a treatment. Not because it is painful, but because it makes them focus on emotional blockages. It truly helps clear all the chakras and energy channels. It can be an overwhelming experience for some people."

"People really cry during a treatment?" Lily had never thought about reflexology in this way, but thinking back to her Reiki training she understood how it was possible.

"I have one client that doesn't cry, but this lady, who is in her seventies is so in tuned with her body that she can tell me which body part I am working on when I put pressure on parts of her feet. She will say, 'My teeth are tingling.' Or 'I feel that in my spine.' It is amazing just how she can pinpoint each nerve center with the corresponding body part without having any prior knowledge." Glen dried Lily's feet and led her to the treatment chair. Lily sat down and her feet were raised up and rested on a pillow. One foot was wrapped in a towel and Glen started the treatment on the other. At first Lily just relaxed into the treatment which felt like a very good foot massage but after a few minutes she started to feel some strange sensations come over her body.

"Can I talk during the treatment or would you rather I didn't?" she asked. Why did she feel so strange?

"Do whatever feels right." Glen continued to work in silence.

After twenty minutes, Lily realized that tears were streaming down her face. She felt very sad. "What are you thinking about Lily?" His voice was very soft and soothing. Just the sound of his voice enveloped her in a calming, secure blanket.

"For some reason, I am thinking about my father." She felt strange telling him this.

"You have not mourned your father yet Lily."

"What did you say?" How did he know about her father? "I want to stop now!" Lily was confused. What was happening here?

"No Lily, close your eyes and relax. Please Lily, do as I say." Again, his voice calmed her. She closed her eyes. "Now see your father." Before she could resist, with eyes closed, she saw her father right in front of her.

"I see him, he is really here." Lily's voice was as quiet as a whisper.

"Now take the time to really say goodbye Lily, you have all the time in the world. You are safe here." Glen continued to do the reflexology treatment on Lily's feet. She remained eyes closed, tears flowing for several minutes. She felt real sorrow, deep seated grief as she finally said goodbye to her father.

Afterwards Lily told Glen that she could not believe the effect the treatment had on her. She was very grateful. Glen reminded her that emotions buried can cause many problems both physical and emotional and this was a good way to clear her mind and her chakras. Now he recommended a three-day detox to complete the treatment. Lily left, determined to learn all she could about healthy eating and to continue her journey to health, spirit and emotional well- being. She slipped out of the bookstore without seeing Nicole, Lily needed time to herself to absorb what had just happened.

She walked along Water Street to the waterfront, where she found a secluded park bench. Lily sat and stared into the water. She felt lighter, filled with new energy and love. She was very glad that she had not cancelled her appointment with Glen. He was a gifted healer.

Chapter Six

Later that night, Lily told Keith about her reflexology treatment. "Maybe you should make an appointment. I can't believe how much better I feel now, Keith. Glen could probably help you with your issues with the past." She looked at him hopefully.

"I don't think so Lily, let's take this one step at a time. I am jogging every day, and I have lost twelve pounds. It really helps with the stress. So please, let me focus on one improvement at a time, okay?" He squeezed her hand.

"Okay, I just thought I would mention it. Would you like a cup of chamomile tea before bed?" Lily went to the kitchen. She was going to do the detox that Glen suggested for three days and then start making only very healthy meals for her family. Keith was losing weight and she knew that good organic foods would only help that situation. The children needed good food to grow and be healthy and although she had always tried to feed them properly. Now Lily was determined to make a real difference.

Lily spent the next few weeks clearing the house of anything that didn't fit her new diet regime. She had taken a nutrition course a few years ago and always made sure there was no junk food in the house but now she was going to get serious. She didn't want to go totally vegan, but she was going to restrict meat to fish or chicken and turkey, and organic free- range meats only. Lots of fruits and vegetables that she would purchase at the Farmer's market or from the organic section of the grocery store would complete their menu. At first the kids complained, but they soon found their favorite fruits and vegetables and Celeste even brought home a book on the health of our planet and how each person could make a difference. It became a family project and Lily was delighted.

Blane did a school project on recycling which surprised Lily very much. It was amazing the things he came up with on how to use and reuse just about everything. The teacher was so impressed, she made it an assignment for the entire class and told Keith and Lily about it at parent teacher night. Even Keith started contributing to the menu with new healthy ideas. Life was changing for the better in Lily's home.

Nicole and Glen started dating and Lily was thrilled. She decided to invite them over for a bar-b-que on the weekend. Keith was fine with Glen, now that he was dating Nicole. "I hope the entire conversation won't be healthy eating and alternative therapy. I won't be able to add much to that." Keith commented while they waited for their guests to arrive.

"Don't be silly, Nicole can talk about anything. You know how intelligent she is and Glen is the same. You will have no problem. Now go and tell the kids to get ready, the guests should be here any minute." Lily just laughed. She hadn't observed Keith's insecurities like this before.

"Lily, Keith, thank you so much for the invitation. Lily I love that skirt!" Nicole and Glen arrived on time. Lily was wearing a long, loose skirt of soft green. Her white blouse had full sleeves and she was wearing a necklace of tourmaline and green amethyst. She thanked her friend and returned the compliment. Nicole wore brown capris, leather sandals and a brightly colored t-shirt. Both women loved fashion and always looked well put together.

The afternoon went very well. Glen and Keith discovered that they both loved golf and spent most of the time discussing who would win the Ryder Cup or who would be number one at the end of the season. Nicole and Lily were pleased to see the two men getting along so well.

"Glen and Keith seem to be hitting it off." Nicole picked up a piece of watermelon from the dish.

"Golf is a wonderful equalizer." Lily laughed reaching for the watermelon. She took a bite and the moist melon spilled out over her chin. Luckily, she leaned forward just in time to save her white blouse from stains. Nicole laughed loudly.

"No more for you sloppy!" Lily and Nicole chuckled at Lily's blunder.

"Take your shirt off Mommy, then you won't get stains!" Blane shouted from the left.

"I don't think that would be appropriate young man." Lily teased.

"What a little monkey!" Nicole nodded in agreement.

"It's a good thing Conrad isn't here. He has trouble with our double standard of discipline between his mother's house and ours. I don't know what he would think about that comment."

"Is he okay?" Nicole settled in the Muskoka chair next to Lily.

"He is, but sometimes I think it's hard for him. We do things differently and now with the new eating regime, he is really finding things difficult."

"You will handle it, you always manage to find a way to get through to your kids. Sometimes I am amazed at how normal you and your family are, considering your healing talents and your daily dealings with all the different clients and their problems. Not to mention Keith's childhood experiences and yours as well. You really amaze me, Lily. I would never have been able to be a parent."

"Didn't you ever want children, Nicole?"

"Nope, never. Not my scene. I love my privacy, my freedom and my space. No kids for me. And the good thing about Glen is, he feels the same."

"Do you know that as a teenager, I said I would never have kids. I didn't realize how much pleasure or how much fear they would inflict on me. But now I wouldn't change it for the world. I love all three of them with all my heart. Now speaking of Glen, how is this new relationship going? You two seem very well suited."

"I like Glen. He is easy to be with and he is very intelligent. We have conversations about the strangest things, space, psychology, history, just about anything. He is very stimulating to be with."

"Did he tell you what happened when I had my treatment with him?"

"No, Glen never discusses his patients. That is confidential, but you told me it was a real awakening for you. I am glad Lily. You help so many people, it is good that you have found someone to help you. Anymore treatments in the near future? Or how about Keith, would he go?"

"Not yet, but maybe now that he has spent time with Glen there is hope. It would really do him a lot of good. But I can't push him. He is doing so well with the jogging and that was Conrad's doing, not mine."

Glen and Keith were kicking the soccer ball with Blane and Celeste. Everyone had an enjoyable afternoon.

When the kids were in bed and the guests had gone, Keith could not stop talking about what a great guy Glen was. Lily was very pleased. She almost mentioned a reflexology treatment but decided to leave it. Keith would go in his own time.

The following day, Lily had only one client, a gentleman. Mr. Borgen arrived precisely on time. Lily made him a cup of tea and directed him to one of the chairs.

"Have you been to someone like me before?"

"No, I kinda know what you do but my wife couldn't tell me everything, she just wanted me to come. She thought you could do something for me or us." He looked down at his hands.

"I will begin by telling you what I do. I am a healer, an empath, an intuitive, a medium and a life coach. I use my gifts to help others get to the core issues that may be stopping them from moving forward. I help with answers that I receive from your guides and helpers from the other side." She watched his face as she explained. He was listening, that was a good start. "Now how can I help you today.?"

"Well I'm not sure where to begin." Once again, he focused on his hands. He wouldn't look at Lily.

"Let's just talk until you feel comfortable, maybe begin when you are ready."

"I cheated on my wife," he blurted. "She is still having trouble with it and it affects our relationship. I'm not sure what to do to help her." He looked up.

"Is it over with this other person for good?" He nodded in the affirmative. "First I have to ask. Do you still want to be in the marriage?"

"Yes."

"Do you still feel guilty?"

"Yes, I do."

"I want to explain just how I see how things like this happen. The affair, no matter what you may think, lack of attention, sex, lack of time together; none of this is why you did it. Do you understand?

"Yes. Because I just fell into it."

"Actually, no you didn't. When you feel within yourself, that you are not good enough or can't seem to fulfill yourself in some area, you will then go outside of yourself to look for an ego boost, some attention to make you feel better. Some people find it in a job, some find it through another person. It doesn't matter how, it matters why. Lack of self- worth and self -esteem lead you astray and suddenly you feel stronger, more confident when someone else wants you. You begin to fill yourself up with confidence. Am I right?"

"Exactly."

"Are you seeking help for this part of yourself?"

"Yes, we are seeing a marriage therapist but it's not working for me. I mean, I talk and share but I need something more to help me not feel so bad when I look at her. The guilt is eating me up."

"The energy of guilt looks for punishment. When we feel guilty, someone will enter your life and give you a hard time about something to make your life miserable. This can repeat over and over for years because we cannot forgive ourselves.

"Here is what you can do. We are going to do two things here to help you, help your wife and you and your marriage. Would you like to try it?" Mr. Borgen agrees wholeheartedly,
"I am going to take you back to the time you made the decision to have the affair. Then I am going to take you back to another memory. Are you ready?"

"Oh yeah anything that can help, this all sucks."

"Let's begin. This will be visualization. Close your eyes and take a full deep breath. Hold, release, hold, release and now take another one but this time hold it as long as you can. Now let go, please take another breath and hold, hold, now let go. One more, take a breath, from deep in the belly and hold it and then let go. Now I want you to go to the moment when you were with this person, can you see her?"

"Yes."

"I want you to tell her this is a mistake. Tell her it won't turn out well for you, so you are choosing not to do this. Add anything else you would like to say to her and then let me know when you are done."

Lily goes to make more tea leaving Mr. Borgen alone. After about five minutes he says he is good. "Say goodbye, come back to this room and open your eyes, how do you feel?"

"Different, calmer, even though I did it, it feels like I changed it."

"Yes, now we need to do something else. Sit for a few minutes quietly." Lily lets him sit, eyes closed for about three minutes to let him fully integrate. She tells him to breath and hold it several times.

"Let go. Now I want you to see yourself at your wedding, taking your vows with your wife. This time, I want you to say your truth as you know it now. Express the love you now have for her, deeper love. Hold her hands, look into her eyes. I will give you a moment to do this. Please, let me know when you are done." This time he is silent for about eight minutes. Lily sips her tea and waits. When he indicates he is done, she adds, "Tell her, I free you, I no longer feel the guilt that prevents us from being close again. I love you. Now walk together into this new life and visualize how it looks now, happy, free, full of laughter, and love. When you are done open your eyes." She waits, "How do you feel?"

"Feel better, I feel like it will be different. Looks brighter in here." He looks around like he is seeing it for the first time.

Lily laughs, "Yes that's good. Now let me say this: Guilt has no purpose, when you are connected to your partner, you feel each other. The connection is deep between people. There is a telepathy that happens. Have you ever thought something like, "I'd like to go to the movies" for instance and then she says, 'Hey want to go to the movies or go out?' This is because the message has been sent to her on that level. Now think about guilt, which is a negative energy. When you feel it, have you noticed that is when she suddenly remembers something you did in the past and starts asking you questions again, or gets angry or depressed?"

"Yes, I have. It's funny you should say that, just yesterday I was at work and couldn't stop thinking about it.

I felt bad and very guilty. It was just all too confusing. I couldn't shake it off."

"How was it when you got home?"

"It was bad, I knew as soon as I walked in, she was also having a bad day."

"Now you know why, it is the connection, telepathy. Therefore, your marriage would not be able to heal if you kept on doing this. This is why most marriages cannot survive something like this. Do you understand?"

"Yes!"

"Guilt is a funny thing. A little may guide us. but a lot destroys us and everything we have. Think about your wife and the affair going home. How do you feel?"

"Great! I feel different about it all. I know I can do this for her."

"I want to add something for her. You must allow her to have her feelings. These are hers, let her have them. They are not about you and she will move through this faster if you do not make it about you. We all attract who we need in our lives to help us learn and grow, you two can do this. But now you need to give her what she needs and it will end and you can get back to a better deeper relationship."

How do you feel about this? Can you do this for her?"

"Absolutely." Lily sits quietly allowing Mr. Borgen to make the move to leave. She knows he is assimilating all the knowledge, which is not common therapy but works immediately. After about 5 minutes he leans forward.

"Are you okay? You are ready to work with all this?"

"Yes, thank you so much." They stand and he hugs Lily. "I can't believe how much better I feel. Thank you, Lily." He hands her a check and turns to leave.

"Take care of yourself, and live a long, happy life." After he left Lily realized she didn't have a brochure for guilt. She would speak to Nicole, she really liked giving the clients something to take with them.

Chapter Seven

It was Saturday morning and Glen arrived to pick up Keith for a game of golf. Lily was very pleased that Keith was taking some time for himself. "Hi Lily, is Keith ready?"

"He's in the garage Glen. How are things?" Lily put the dishes in the cupboard as she chatted. "Thanks for inviting him, he really needs to relax more."

"Golf can be a very relaxing pass time or a totally stressed out day!" Glen chuckled.

"It better be relaxing!" Keith walked in the kitchen. 'Hi Glen, ready to go?"

"See you later Lily." Keith gave Lily a peck on the cheek and headed out the door after Glen. She smiled. *Maybe some of Glen's calm demeanor will rub off on you. If only I could break through that wall Keith, I know I could help you.* How many times had she thought about that? *No sense thinking about that now, you have things to do.* She gave herself a shake. Celeste has swimming lessons this morning and Blane was going to a birthday party this afternoon. Lily had things to do and she reminded herself that she better get busy.

Keith arrived home just before dinner. He was quiet but pleased with himself. Lily wondered what he was thinking, he seemed to be contemplating something very serious. "Golf game go well today? Anything interesting happen?" She wanted to know what was on his mind and tried to get him to open up.

"Great, I shot an eighty- five! Glen is a good golfer; much better than I am. He shot seventy- three." Keith set the table carefully. "He is a very interesting person. I don't think I have ever met a guy like him." Keith seemed to return to his far away thoughts, so Lily let it go.

After supper, she got the kids bathed and into bed. She settled in the living room with a glass of red wine. Keith was watching television. "Would you like a glass?"

"I think I'll have a whisky. Turn that off, will you?" Keith went to the sideboard and poured himself a drink. He came back and joined her on the sofa, which Lily found odd because he always sat in his lazy boy chair. She smiled and waited patiently for him to say something. She could feel his energy had shifted. Something must have happened today.

"Glen was telling me about the five truths of Buddhism." Lily looked surprised.
"Glen was saying that life is no picnic. All too often, we have to overcome obstacles in order to survive." He stopped and took a sip of his drink. He let the warming liquid settle in his mouth for a few seconds before swallowing. "According to Glen, sometimes we try to deny these obstacles because they're too difficult to bare. But as hard as they are to confront, it's necessary if we want to live a truly fulfilling and free life."

"That is very true, what else did he say." Lily was trying to suppress her excitement. This was a very big step for Keith. She had never heard him discuss subjects like this before. She drank her wine and waited.

"According to Buddhist philosophy, happiness involves embracing and accepting all the different aspects of life, even the negative. If not, we're turning a blind eye to reality and resisting the natural forces of the universe. What do you think about that?" Keith looked at her curiously.

"I agree totally. Did he say anything else?" She sat up straighter, focusing her attention on Keith. She was hoping he would continue and not close down like he usually did.

"Glen says one of the truths is that worrying is useless." He looked at her and laughed. "Yes, I know you tell me that all the time but it made sense the way he put it." She reached for his hand and he continued. "Worrying does not accomplish anything. Even if you worry twenty times, it won't change the situation. In fact, your anxiety will only make things worse."

Lily agreed, "Yes, even though things are not as we would like, we can still be content, knowing we are trying our best and will continue to do so."

"Glen quoted some Buddhist, Thich Nhat Hanh, 'The most important practice is aimlessness, not running after things, not grasping.' I don't know why but that really hit home with me. I feel like I am constantly running after things and getting nowhere." He looked away, a faraway look in his eyes. Lily sat back and waited. This was a huge breakthrough for Keith, she was very thankful to Glen. Although she wanted to say so much, to encourage this new way of thinking, she knew Keith and she knew she would have to leave it with him for now.

"I'm going to bed now Keith, are you coming?"

"No, I'm going to sit here for a little while. Good night Lily." She bent down and kissed his cheek.

"Good night, Keith." Lily could feel the positive energy coming from him. She was very happy.

Monday morning, Lily stopped by the bookstore before going up to her office. Nicole and Glen were sharing a coffee and deep in conversation. "Good morning, you two. Hope I'm not interrupting." Lily laughed.

"No, grab a coffee and join us. Busy day?" Nicole smiled.

"Glen, thanks for taking Keith golfing. He came home in a very good mood." Lily decided not to discuss Keith's new way of thinking, but wanted to say thank you.

"He is a great guy. Listen Lily, we were just discussing some seminars that I am going to give here in the bookstore. Nicole suggested that you might like to do a couple."

"I would love to hear you speak, Glen." Lily let the aroma of the freshly brewed coffee fill her nostrils. What a glorious smell. She would like to attend Glen's seminars and maybe now, Keith would join her.

"No, I mean you come as the speaker. Talk about what you do and how it helps people. It would be great for business." Lily looked up in surprise.

"Me?" She set her cup down before it spilled.

"Why not? You are a gifted healer and you could talk about being an empath, and an intuitive. Many people would be very interested, Lily." Nicole added.

"I never thought about doing speaking engagements before. Let me think about it. But Glen, I would still like to come and hear you speak. Keep me posted on the details."

"The bookstore is going to become a beehive of activity in Gastown." Nicole beamed. "We will have people lining up for seminars soon." Nicole and Glen seemed to have an excellent rapport, both personal and professional. They worked well together.

"I will leave you two alone to conjure up more brilliant ideas, I have clients to see. Bye for now." Lily stood up and walked toward the door. "Oh, by the way, did that book for Celeste come yet? She is really into this 'Save the Planet' mode and asks me every day."

"Not yet, but the shipment is due anytime. I'll let you know as soon as it comes. Oh, grab that pile of brochures on the table. I printed them last night. Bye Lily." Lily picked up the brochures, and thanked her friend.

Upstairs Lily sorted the brochures into piles for the clients, this was one idea of Nicole's that had made a big hit with Lily's clients. When she saw the one titled, 'The Five Truths of Buddhism,' she smiled. Looks like Glen had some influence on the brochures as well. Lily poured herself a cup of tea and settled in her big leather chair with the brochure. She read:

1) Worrying is useless.

Worrying is created in the mind and really doesn't offer any value to our lives. Will worrying change what's going to happen? If not, then it's a waste of time. As Buddhist master Thich Nhat Hanh says, try to remain in the present moment without putting labels on your "future conditions of happiness."

If we don't know how to breathe, smile, and live every moment of our life deeply, we will never be able to help anyone.

2) If we want to be happy, we must see reality for what it is

Buddhism teaches us that we must see reality for what it is if you want to be truly free. Instead of being fixed on our ideas and opinions, we need to stay open and curious to whatever truth arises.

So many of us try to remain perpetually positive by avoiding negative emotions or situations. But we need to confront them and accept them if we are to be truly free.

3) We need to accept change actively

Everything in life is change. You're born and you eventually die. The weather changes every day. No matter how you look at life, everything is change. However, many of us attempt to keep things "fixed" and "constant". But this only goes against the true forces of the universe.

By accepting and embracing change, it gives us enormous liberation and energy to create the lives we want.

4) The root of suffering is pursuing temporary feelings

So many of us crave those feelings of what we think is happiness. We think happiness includes excitement, joy, euphoria...but these are only temporary feelings. And the constant pursuit of these feelings only turns into suffering because they don't last.

Instead true happiness comes from inner peace – being content with what you have and who you are.

5) Meditation is the path to reducing suffering
Meditation teaches us that everything is impermanent, especially our feelings. It teaches us that the present moment is all that exists. And when we truly realize that, we become content and happy.

Now Lily understood why Glen had been able to reach Keith. He presented him with just enough information to raise his curiosity without overload or any burden of acting. Glen simply planted the seed and left Keith to make it grow. Her respect for Glen was growing. Not only had he helped her, but now he was helping Keith. She would take this brochure home and leave it somewhere inconspicuous for Keith to find.

Lily realized it was almost ten o'clock and her first client would be arriving any minute. A quick bathroom pit stop and she would be ready.

A woman in her thirties arrived, looking tired, worried and very pregnant. She was frantic, pregnant with her 3rd child. It wasn't about having another child, it was about the pain she endured during her pregnancies. Previous pregnancies had resulted in bed rest because of back pain and nausea. She explained to Lily that she wanted to be excited but was afraid of what would happen again.

Lily asked her to sit down. Her name was Millie. She was 5 months pregnant and desperate to see if anything Lily did could help. The baby was sitting on her spine causing tremendous pain and she was told by her doctor that she will have to go on bed rest.

Lily asked her to come over to the massage table in the corner and lay down. Millie hesitated but complied. Lily began, "I want you to relax, breathe and just see your connection with her baby. May I touch you?" Millie nodded, very curious about what Lily would do.

Lily laid her hands on her stomach, and could feel the baby. As Lily connected with the baby, she asked the child to move slightly and to follow her hands, she projected thoughts to the child explaining that her mommy was hurting because of where she was laying. As Lily moved her hands, slowly the baby followed. She moved right off of Millie's spine."

Millie gasped. "The baby just moved. Oh my God, the pain has subsided! It is there but much better, duller and I feel such relief. What did you do?" Millie was very impressed but confused.

Lily explained, "We tend to make everything so hard and yet why not just ask? We are deeply connected to one another in the womb. We are one. When we listen, we will hear. In the womb, babies, and toddlers up to the age of 9 are openly connected to the spirit world. Fear from parents and others can change that in us, but it is always there to reconnect to. I simply connected with your baby and asked the child to move so that you would not suffer. Don't be afraid to speak by telepathy with your child, he or she can hear you."

Millie climbed down from the massage table with ease, she could not believe the difference in her back pain. "Thank you so much Lily, you are a gifted healer. I will be sure and tell all of my friends about you."

When Millie left, Lily sat and pondered life for a few minutes before the next client. She knew that she could hear the universe speak to her. She knew that if she was in the moment, she could receive messages from everywhere. She trusted that where she was and what she was doing, was exactly where she needed to be. If only more people would just listen!

Chapter Eight

Lily opened her eyes, the sun was filtering through the curtains and she could hear voices downstairs. Rolling over she glanced at the clock, seven thirty, the numbers glowed back at her. *Oh my, I must have slept in.* As was her habit, Lily lay on her back and repeated her daily prayer*: Allow me to see what I must see. Hear what I must hear and feel what I must feel. Help me to see through the illusions and see the real wonders of the world. Amen.* The prayer helped her to stay focused and be mindful. With a smile on her lips, Lily sat up and stretched. Today she was staying home to catch up on some housework. Her day would be a wonderful adventure, she would make it happen.

By the time Lily arrived in the kitchen, the kids were on their way out the door to school and Keith was already gone. "Did you two have a good breakfast?"

"Yes, Daddy made us eggs and toast soldiers. Bye Mommy, love you." Celeste was out the door before Lily could kiss her goodbye. She helped Blane with his backpack and kissed the top of his head.

"Have a wonderful day, Blane. I will pick you up after your practice. I am sure you will get a good part in the play." Blane smiled his big wide grin. The boy was a born actor.

Lily spent the morning doing laundry and cleaning up the house. She was meeting a friend for lunch at twelve and took a quick shower. She put chicken and vegetables in her crock pot for supper and left the house, she felt content and happy.

Lily's friend Jane was already at the restaurant when Lily arrived. Jane was a lawyer, very well dressed and her hair was always perfectly coiffed. Lily wore a flowing flowered skirt, sandals and a peasant blouse. She was in a free and easy mood and just wanted to dress to match how she felt. "Jane, so good to see you. Have you been here long."

"No, not long. You look very perky and carefree today, Lily."

"And you look like a very successful lawyer, as usual. How is the practice going?"

"It is going almost too well, I need to hire another attorney. That however, is not going well." Jane looked at the menu, and Lily thought something was bothering her friend but decided to let it go.

It took several minutes for Jane to decide, she seemed unable to focus, "I can't decide, just bring me the fish and a Greek salad." Jane spoke to the waiter without looking up. "How about you Lily?"

"Sounds delicious, now tell me all about your life since I saw you last."

The two women chatted for two hours, drank coffee and then did a little shopping together. After Jane climbed into her taxi, Lily continued doing her errands but her mood was decidedly off. She felt much different than this morning. Something was wrong. She walked into a trash can on the sidewalk and bruised her knee. *Yikes, Lily what is the matter with you! Jane was obviously depressed and giving off her energy and you didn't pay attention. Now you have picked up all her depressed energy and hurt yourself.* Lily reprimanded herself. She knew better, she was an empath and picking up other people's emotions and energy were common. She walked into the closest café and ordered a coffee. She needed to collect and clear herself of Jane's energy. Lily knew she had to keep herself in the moment and listen. An hour later she felt much better and continued her afternoon in a happy mood. *This isn't always easy, even for me.*

It had been weeks since Keith and Glen had gone golfing and Lily was noticing an improvement in Keith's disposition. She believed they could make some real breakthroughs if this continued. Lily loved Keith, but sometimes he could be very difficult.

That evening he arrived home in a foul mood. A big contract he was working on had fallen through and it meant a lot of work to recover. He refused to eat his dinner and went to the living room to be alone. Lily explained to the kids that Daddy was having a bad day, and it was best to leave him alone for tonight.

Blane was oblivious to anything but his part in the new play. "I will be an old man, with a cane. I have to practice." After his meal, he climbed down from his chair, bent over and shuffled slowly from the room, leaving Celeste and Lily laughing at him.

"What a dork!" Celeste could stop laughing. "He even looks like an old man."

"I brought the new book home yesterday, it is on the counter." Celeste leapt up at the mention of a new book and quickly reached for it.

"Thanks Mom. Now I can learn about climate change and global warming. I'll be upstairs." Lily just shook her head. When Celeste latched on to something, she was like a dog with a bone. Nothing could pry her away from her new interest. Lily cleared the table, not looking forward to an evening with Keith. His moods could be very unnerving and after her slip with Jane, Lily was not going to let his energy affect her.

It was eight o'clock when Lily finally joined Keith in the living room. She poured a glass of wine and settled on the couch. The silence covered them like a blanket and Lily remained at peace.

"Today was hell." Keith turned off the television and turned toward Lily. She was surprised but determined to stay focused. She was not sure if the three whiskeys had loosened his lips or if he genuinely wanted to share his day, but Lily was careful not to interrupt. Keith told her about the contract and how it had gone bad. He explained how much difficulty this was going to cause him at work and how worried he was.

Lily switched to healer mode, "Could I make a suggestion?"

"Sure, it can't get any worse." Keith sat looking at his hands.

"If you want things to go smoothly at work, perhaps you could spend some time thinking and actually seeing it going smoothly. Go into work calm and collected and see it go smoothly."

"And when the shit hits the fan!" Keith wasn't really receptive but Lily carried on.

"When something goes wrong just look at it calmly and decide that it will work itself out, just let it go. If you focus on yourself and keep reminding yourself that you are calm and everything is going smoothly, things will take a turn for the better. You will see how easy it comes to you if you just try."

"I hear what you are saying, but I don't think I can do that. Things need to be done or everything will go wrong!"

"If you expect everything to go wrong, it will. Is it your ego that needs to feel needed? Ego can be very sneaky, it wants to feel important. If you can address this issue, perhaps you can just let things go and focus on everything going smoothly."

"Oh, this is too much work! I am in a crisis at work. I don't have time to worry about my ego!" Keith was growing more agitated.

Just plant the seed and walk away, Lily could hear the words over and over in her mind.

"If you can choose to think positively, how you look at the situation will change the situation. But if you let your ego get in the way, you will lose. Train yourself to think positively and if negativity pops up, correct it immediately." Lily finished her wine.

"All of this is easy for you. I can't just change how I think, unlearn how to react!"

Lily stood up, "Goodnight Keith." She walked out of the room leaving him watching her go. He slept on the couch.

Lily stopped in to see Glen the next morning. "Hi Glen, I have been thinking about the seminars and I think I would like to give it a try. I could do one on energy, would that be okay?"

Lily had been thinking about becoming a speaker and this was an opportunity she didn't want to ignore. However, she was still intimidated by the idea of standing up in front of a group of people and speaking.

"Energy would be perfect, Lily. I will schedule you in. Are you free most evenings?" Glen was already writing in the planner, no getting out of it now.

"Sure, any evening would work. Will you give me some notice?"

"Of course, my seminars are starting next week, Tuesday and Thursday. If you and Keith would like to come, I can save you a couple of seats. I have thirty- five signed up already."

Lily wasn't sure about Keith but she wanted to attend, "Put us down for a Tuesday session, that is the best night for us because I can get Mrs. Carter to stay with the kids."

Lily left Glen and went up to her office. She was hoping that some of the information she gave to Keith would help, but he didn't seem that receptive. She would have to be patient.

The phone rang just as she sat in her chair. "Hello?"

"Lily, I want to apologize for last night. I decided to try your theory of positive thinking and so far, this morning is going well. I love you Lily, I really am sorry." Lily was astonished.

"I am so glad you decided to give it a try. Just keep correcting yourself if you feel yourself slipping back into a negative energy. Call me if you need to. I love you too, Keith." Lily hung up and sat back to absorb what had just happened. The seed was actually taking root! Perhaps the previous weeks of thinking about the five truths of Buddhism, combined with last night's little pep talk was taking shape in Keith's mind. She would definitely try to convince him to attend Glen's seminar. *Just be careful, move slowly. One step at a time. Be patient.* Lily's angels were on duty to remind her to go slow.

Lily was thinking about Keith when a young man appeared at her door. "Hello?"

"Hello, come in please." Lily was confused because her next patient wasn't due until eleven and this young man was definitely not Mrs. Grey. He was about nineteen years old, with shaggy brown hair falling into his eyes. Lily noticed his eyes right away, they were sad. "What can I do for you today?"

Looking confused and depressed, he looked at her. "I'm not sure. I'm not sure I believe in any of this. I was in the bookstore downstairs and they told me about you."

"That's okay, what is it that I might be able to help you with?" The boy shrugged. "How about we talk for a bit and see what happens." Lily could see the young man was very troubled.

"I...I had a best friend. We were really close. One night we got together and we did some drugs." He looked at Lily but saw no judgement on her face, he continued. "We tried to commit a pact suicide." The young man looked away. "The only thing is; that he died and I didn't." He broke down. Lily let him cry.

"Within minutes she felt a presence. A spiritual presence was coming through very strongly. "His name is Matt?"

"Yes!" The young man, whose name was Bill looked very surprised.

"He is here." Lily waited a few seconds, she closed her eyes. "He wants you to know it's okay. He is okay and you are okay. Matt says it is good that you are alive."

Bill grew very angry, "No! It's not okay. He should be alive!" Bill was very upset. He pulled his knees up to his chest in a fetal position, his head was covered by his arm as if he wanted to hide. He sobbed and cried.

Lily tried to tell him Matt was not angry with him, but he wouldn't have it.

"I'm not sure I believe in this shit anyway." Bill jumped up, he was angry and filled with guilt.

Lily replied, "No problem but spirit will show you this is real, Bill. Spirit will make sure you see its all real."

He didn't believe her and rushed out the door. She could hear his feet pounding the stairs as he fled.

Lily was very upset, tears rolled down her cheeks. She was filled with a great sadness as she remembered her own suicide attempt. Lily was only sixteen and at her lowest point of her young life. She had been molested by a trusted relative, her parents were fighting, her home life was in shreds and she was failing miserable at school. She could almost feel the sadness, the loneliness that sixteen-year old Lily had felt. It was a sense of total desperation. It seemed she had no other choice. Fortunately for Lily, her sister saw her go into the bathroom. She sensed something was wrong and followed Lily. She stopped her from taking her life that fateful day.

Now, many years later, Lily realized that it was a learning and growing experience and that she had to let go of her past in order to see her life differently. It had been a very long journey to the woman she was today. Lily was thankful to the young man for reminding her how wonderful her life was now. She was very grateful to be alive and very grateful to be able to use her own suffering to help so many people. Lily put the old memories to the back of her mind and thought of Bill. *I hope he comes back. He needs help and I understand.*

Two weeks later, Keith got tickets to a basketball game. They had never gone to one and Celeste really wanted to go. Lily decided to get a hotel in the city and make it a little get away for the family. Celeste was so excited.

They arrived at the hotel, hungry and tired. "Let's get something to eat," Lily proposed.

Keith suggested room service, and they ordered what they wanted. An hour later, there was a knock at the door. Lily opened the door and who was standing there with wide brown eyes, looking more confused than Lily? Bill. She was quickly reminded that spirit had said he would be shown this is all real. She was surprised but all she could do was laugh.

"This is too funny, you work here?"

"Yes," he said, "I don't usually deliver food to the rooms but the regular guy was busy. Can I come in?" He laughed. Keith, Blane and Celeste all looked on curiously as Bill pushed the food cart into the room.

Even Lily was amazed how spirit works. He left shaking his head and Lily explained to Keith what Bill's story was. He just stared at her in awe. "And now you run into him at the hotel? That is weird!" The children ate with gusto, not interested in the hotel employee or his story.

A week later, Bill called asking if he could see Lily. She agreed and when he arrived, he was more willing to talk and start the process of healing. During the appointment, he said he was blown away when he saw her. He took that as a sign from Matt and wanted to know more

They talked about the suicide and why Matt died. Lily explained that she believes we never go until we need to, as strange as that sounds. "Matt was done with his time on earth, you are not. The two of you came together to make something happen. In this life, things don't always look the way we think they should. He will be with you and help you now from a special place." Bill looked much more at peace than he had before.

"Thank you, Lily, you have made me see that I have a special purpose here and that Matt will guide me to that purpose. You have made a believer out of me." Bill left, but called Lily a few weeks later and told her he had a job working with troubled teens. Lily was thrilled.

Chapter Nine

Keith came home in a foul mood. The new territorial CEO had been chosen and it was someone Keith did not like. The man was an ego maniac with little empathy for the workers. Keith was not looking forward to working with him. After dinner, Lily sat with him and tried to open a dialogue, Keith was silent.

"You have options, Keith. Why don't we discuss what changes you might make at work?"

"Options! Changes! Maybe I'll just quit and we will all be homeless! I have a mortgage to pay, a family to support. I don't have options!" He grew angrier with each sentence.

"I understand all of that, but perhaps you are letting this guy's negativity get to you."

"The guy's negativity has nothing to do with it. My job could be in jeopardy and all of this 'Don't worry, stay positive crap' will not help me. Lily, just please leave me alone." He poured another whisky and left the room. Lily didn't know whether to follow him or leave him alone as he asked. She wanted to help but unless Keith was willing to talk, there was nothing she could do. Keith's past made him hard wired to social pressures of work, money and caring for his family. His mother raised him in fear and he always made safe choices. She thought Glen may have made some inroads with Keith, but it looked like he had reverted to his old ways once again. She poured a glass of wine and sat in the living room alone. Lily looked upon Keith's job as a jungle, filled with hungry animals trying to devour each other. It was a world she had moved past quite a while ago. Now she had to help Keith move forward into the spiritual world and away from the jungle, but how? All of Lily's life experiences had led her here. She understood how many of her clients felt and she believed that everyone can heal, however first they have to ask for help, that was the hardest part. When would Keith ask for help?

The next morning, Keith went into the office, even though it was Saturday. Lily didn't question him, she just let him go. Celeste was next door playing with her friend, Joanie. Lily didn't know the Martins very well. They had only moved in about two months ago but Celeste and Joanie seemed to hit it off right away. Joanie was a very polite and obedient child. Lily did notice that the Martins were very religious and in her opinion, controlling. The children were not allowed to speak their minds or show frustration.

Celeste returned an hour later and when Lily asked her a question, Celeste shouted at her. This was very uncharacteristic of Celeste, but Lily noticed that every time she was with Joanie, she seemed to throw a tantrum. Now Lily understood that Celeste was picking up Joanie's energy, the suppressed energy of a controlled environment and releasing it for her. Celeste obviously had some of her Mother's ability as an empath. Lily just let Celeste be and soon it was over. Now she would have to figure out how to explain to her daughter what was happening.

Celeste took her book and went to her room leaving Lily remembering how she herself picked up energy as a child. Lily was a difficult child in the opinion of her parents and family. Moody and sensitive and on the inside, she was always second guessing herself. Wondering why she felt the way she did in certain situations. She remembered when she was ten years old, she went to her first funeral. She sat near the front and although she didn't really know this person well, she started to cry, sobbing uncontrollably. At the time, she didn't understand what was happening. Her mother removed her because she was making a scene and disturbing everyone. Lily remembered not understanding why everyone wasn't crying. She felt their sadness deeply and it was overwhelming. Now after many years of research and learning, she understood. She could see the same things happening with Celeste.

Lily went upstairs to Celeste's room and knocked gently. "May I come in?"

"Sure." Celeste was lying on the bed, reading her book. She looked up, wide eyed, "Sorry about the fit, I don't know why I screamed at you like that. Sorry Mom." She could see Celeste was sincere but also confused.

"Listen Honey, I want to talk to you about that. Sometimes we can pick up energy from other people and it makes us feel strange or act out. It is known as empathy, or being an empath. I won't confuse you with all the details, but I have that ability and it is how I can help so many people. I believe you have it too and that is why you acted the way you did." She sat beside her daughter and gently pushed her hair back from her face, "You were picking up the tension from poor Joanie, who I know would love to just scream and release. She can't, so you did it for her. Cats often do this for their owners. They take the tension and stress and release it, just like you did. Do you understand?"

"Sort of. So, Joanie was feeling all tense and stuff and because her parents don't let her yell and scream, I did it for her? Is that what you mean?" Celeste sat up, crossed legged on the bed.

"Yes, you know I love you very much and I am here for you if you ever want to talk about anything."

"Maybe Joanie should get a cat!" Celeste's suggestion made them both laugh. It broke the tension.

"Joanie's family is different than our family. They have a very strict religious belief system than does not allow for outbursts. We must accept and respect that. I want you to remember this, when you are over there; respect them and their beliefs and the way they chose to raise their children, but try not to pick up all of Joanie's suppressed energy. If you do start to feel strange or as if you can't cope, just come home and we can talk about it. Okay?"

Celeste looked like she understood. "So, this is how you help people? Wow, I never really thought about what you do. Maybe I can help people someday." Lily looked at her daughter thinking, *Perhaps, it will be easier for you having a mother that understands and can help with your feelings. It is a difficult road my darling.* She kissed her daughter's head and left her alone.

Back in the kitchen, Lily made a coffee and took it out on the patio. *What a weekend! At least Celeste listened and seemed to take it all in. Keith is another story. How can I reach him?*

"Hello? Anybody home?" Lily looked up to see Conrad standing in the kitchen.

"Out here." She had almost forgotten that his mother was dropping him off after piano practice. "How was practice?"

"Good, I am learning some Mozart pieces and I am starting to like classical music more and more. Where's Blane?"

"Blane is at a birthday party and Celeste is upstairs reading. Come and sit with me."

"Where's Dad?" Conrad looked around the yard expecting to see Keith.

"He had to go into the office for a little while, he will be back later. So, what's new with you?" Lily was not happy that Keith had left without giving Conrad a thought. She knew how much the youngster loved spending time with his dad.

Conrad dropped into the chair beside Lily, his long legs spread out in front of him "Not much, but I do have a new girlfriend. Her name is Annabelle and she is the most beautiful girl in school." He grinned widely, looking very satisfied with himself.

"Annabelle, but I thought Marlene was the most beautiful girl in school, or was that last week?" Lily teased. Conrad just rolled his eyes and laughed. He was a charming teenager and Lily could see why the girls would be attracted to him.

"Hey Conrad, when did you get here?" Celeste joined them on the patio. The two kids chatted together and Lily left them alone in the yard. She returned to the kitchen and phoned the birthday party to see what time Blane would be ready to pick up.

"Okay Mary, I'll pick him up at three. How is the party going?" Lily talked to Mary for a few minutes and hung up the phone. It rang just as she put it down. "Hello?"

"It's me, tell Conrad I'll be home shortly. Sorry to leave without a word but I had to finish this report. See you later." Keith hung up before Lily could reply. She stared at the phone.

That was short and sweet. I guess he doesn't want to talk right now. Maybe later.

Celeste and Conrad were discussing climate change. Celeste showed him her new book and he was definitely interested. "Wait until I show you what I'm reading." Lily watched as Conrad pulled a book from his backpack. She was surprised when it was a book on world travel.

"One day, I will travel the world," Conrad stated proudly. Celeste looked impressed.

Lily joined the two children. "Conrad, if you want to travel, you should consider taking some languages at school. It will help a great deal." Conrad looked up. The light in his eyes, told Lily that she had just ignited a spark in her step son.

"Spanish! I can take Spanish this year. Thanks Lily, wait until I tell Dad!" The two children quickly became engrossed in the travel book. Lily was pleased, leaving them alone to inspire each other.

Lily tidied up the kitchen and took the chicken out of the freezer for supper. The rest of the morning passed quickly.

Chapter Ten

Early Monday morning, Lily decided to go for a forest hike before her first client. This client had been to see her several months ago but was unable to talk about what was bothering her. She called to schedule another appointment today and Lily needed to clear her mind and her heart. The situation with Keith was bothering her. Over the years, Lily knew that being in nature has the effect of winding you down simply because nature's pace is so much slower than our human-made environment. When you start to observe the pulse and rhythm in nature and take it in, you find that everything takes time. It's a process, change is not immediate. To experience nature, was to experience the greatest diffuser of anxious energy.

Arriving at the trail head, Lily closed her eyes and did a short meditation. She told herself to move her awareness from her head and mind, to her heart or spiritual center. She wanted to see, hear and feel this experience from her heart. Lily had learned long ago that experiencing life from the heart instead of the mind, made everything more vibrant, bigger, more alive. It made her feel one with the universe and everything in it. That is how she wanted this hike to be.

When asked, people would describe the forest as 'green'. Lily walked slowly through the forest and by moving her awareness to her heart, she observed not one shade of green, but dozens. On both sides were shades of deep, dark bottle green, apple green, shades of avocado and the very vibrant, bright lime green of the new shoots. She noticed how the new olive green pine cones, while still attached to the end of the branches were decorated with tiny rivers of sap.

Lily was surrounded by the forest's symphony of sounds. Finches, Cardinals, Jays and sparrows all singing their morning greetings in a blend of glorious tones. In the distance, she could hear the cawing of a crow. A cacophony of sound similar to an orchestra tuning up for a concert. The sound filled her heart with connection to nature.

As she turned the bend on the trail, Lily was greeted by wildflowers lining the trail in Buttercup yellow, Chicory blue, and tall, delicate white, Queen Anne's Lace. The combination of color against the varying green backdrop was stunning. A tiny chipmunk scurried across the trail in front of her, and Lily smiled.

The sun filtered through the trees and Lily stopped to observe the beams of light filled with tiny seeds and specks of dust. The trees cast long shadows in the light of the sun and she found it a beautiful sight. Lily let the experience enfold her, like a blanket of safety and belonging.

Further on she noticed dew drops sparkling like tiny diamonds on the broad, dark green leaves. She stopped and let several drops drip into her open palm. The water was cool against her skin. On her left, bright red raspberries hung heavy on the canes. Lily stopped and picked three big, ripe berries and popped them into her mouth. She let the delicate sweet flavor spread over her tongue, enjoying the delectable taste before swallowing. A tiny sparrow appeared on the canes, helping himself to the delightful berries. "They are delicious," Lily confirmed out loud. The sparrow looked at her for a few seconds and feeling no threat, continued his feast.

After an hour, Lily returned to the trail head satisfied and filled to overflowing with love, gratitude and oneness. Her skin was damp from the moist forest air and she could feel trickles of perspiration on the back of her neck. Bringing her focus back to reality, she glanced at her watch and decided she had time to shower and get to her office for her appointment on time, if she hurried. *Back to reality*, she thought to herself.

When Lily arrived at the office, Nicole was outside the bookstore washing the windows. "Don't you have someone that cleans those windows every week?" Lily inquired.

"I do, but the swallow have decided my eaves are the perfect nesting spot and they leave me little surprises on the glass every morning. You look well rested, have a good night?" Nicole wiped the last of the bird droppings from the glass and dropped the rag into the bucket at her feet.

"Just back from a trail walk, the forest was beautiful today." Lily grinned like a cheshire cat. "I feel amazing!"

"Good for you, you should have called me. I would much rather hike than clean bird pooh!" They both laughed. Glen's car appeared at the curb.

"Good Morning Ladies, you both seem happy this fine morning." He opened the back door and lifted something from the seat. "I picked this up. I think you could sell these in the shop, Nicole." Glen held up a sign made of wood. It was painted a rustic brown in a distressed look and on it was the following:

"Every day, think as you wake up, today I am fortunate to be alive, I have a precious human life, I am not going to waste it. I am going to use all my energies to develop myself, to expand my heart out to others; to achieve enlightenment for the benefit of all beings. I am going to have kind thoughts towards others, I am not going to get angry or think badly about others. I am going to benefit others as much as I can." – The Dalai Lama

Both women nodded in agreement. "That is very profound and yes, I do think we could sell those. Did you get anymore?" Nicole lifted the wall plaque from Glen's hands and held it out in front of her. "I like this. Good shopping Glen, where did you get it?"

"A woman at the market makes them, I have three more in the trunk. I knew you would love them." He moved to the back of the car and Nicole gave Lily a nod and a smile.

"He is getting to know me too well."

"I would love to hang that in my office, so this one is sold." Lily took the plaque from Nicole, turned her back as if wanting to make a quick getaway and shouted over her shoulder, "Thanks Glen, pay you later Nicole." Laughing she disappeared into the stairway.

Upstairs she found the perfect place to hang her latest acquisition and stood back admiring it. It was positioned so that clients would see it when they were sitting in one of the high back chairs. Lily thought the words of wisdom could help so many of her clients.

Charlotte arrived a few minutes later. A teen in blue jeans and a T-shirt stood in the doorway. She was very young, only seventeen. Timidly she knocked on the open door. "Hello?"

"Charlotte, please come in. I am so glad you decided to come back to see me. How are things at home now?" Lily directed Charlotte to the chair. "Would you like some tea?"

"Yes please, I have to apologize for the last time I saw you. I just couldn't put my feelings into words. Thank you for seeing me again." Charlotte looked down at her hands, clenched tightly in her lap. "Things are still bad."

Lily set the tea on the table and turned toward Charlotte, "Let's talk and see where we go? Okay?"

Charlotte took a sip of her tea, seeming to search for the right words. "My home life sucks, my whole life my parents have argued, hit each other and can't even see what it does to us kids!" She took a long deep breath, "I don't like going home but until I turn 18 I can't leave, I tried running away but I don't want to live on the streets." Lily can see the tears forming, she hands her a kleenex, but doesn't interrupt. "My life is hell!"

"I'm so sorry that you are experiencing this but it is more common that you know. You have made a very good first step coming to see me. Has anyone every told you that what your parents are doing is them reacting out of pain. A deep pain, from their past, present and future. When people get this deep in their pain, they do not realize what they are doing to others because they only see the pain they are experiencing. I want you to know this before we go any further." Lily let's this sink in for a few seconds as she takes a sip of tea.

"No one ever told me this before!" Charlotte is angry, "But they are the adults!" She doesn't want to hear any excuses for her parents' behavior. Lily realizes she must go slowly.

"Yes, they are, however inside they are not. They are coming from a tiny place inside of them that never healed. They were never loved or accepted and they have no idea how to love or what love looks like. I realize this makes life very difficult for you and your siblings."

"It is just so frustrating! How am I supposed to deal with this?" Lily looked at Charlotte with empathy, she too had a turbulent childhood. She understood the pain and frustration that the young woman was facing.

"Understanding this part usually helps us get to a place within our self that we understand several things. First, it's not about us. Second, we can't do anything for them. Third, we can only help ourselves heal and get strong so we can move on out of this kind of life and not recreate it in our own future. And finally, know this is not love, this is pain." Charlotte gave her a doubtful look. "We can get you to a place where you can at least feel stronger. Help you detach. Would you like that?"

Charlotte pondered what Lily had said for a few moments, "Yes, I just want to feel normal, not scared or angry. Sometimes I feel my anger is getting more and more out of control."

"I want you to tell repeat what I just said to you."

"Okay," her eyes downcast, Lily could see she was struggling. "My parents are in pain. They can't help themselves and I can't help them either." She took a breath, "All this is nothing to do with me, who I am or what I say or do. Is that right?" She looked up at Lily.

"That is right! How does it feel when you say that?" Lily noticed Charlotte sat straighter in her chair, her hands rested on her knees. No longer clenched tightly.

"It feels weird but pretty good at the same time. I feel like I have knowledge something I can work with! Weird. That's it? Just that?" She was looking straight at Lily now, no longer avoiding eye contact.

"Yes, it's a start. We can't do it all today but what would you like to leave here today with?"

"I guess I just want to feel happy? Not angry or scared."

"I would like to share something I learned on my journey that helped me. It's something I believe and when I did it, I moved forward. You see I too had a difficult childhood but after some very hard work and a lot of knowledge seeking, I found some answers that I think will work for you." Lily reached over and took Charlotte's hand. Charlotte's face was filled with questions. "I believe everything we have entered into in this life is a lesson. It's like school. Imagine you are in a large room. A room where souls go to decide what lessons they need to learn during their journey on earth. You say, 'I want to learn to be happy, to be independent and strong.' Then you are shown that in order to learn these things you must enter into a family that will first teach you the feelings of unhappiness, control and weakness." Lily stopped and watched Charlotte absorbing what she was saying. "I want you to think about that for a moment. I will get us more tea." Lily stood up leaving Charlotte to think about all that she had said.

As Lily poured the boiling water into the teapot, Charlotte commented, "I like your sign on the wall." Lily turned toward her.

"I just hung that this morning. I say something very similar every day when I wake up. It sets the tone for the day and it really helps."

"Maybe I'll try that." Charlotte stared at the plaque on the wall until Lily returned.

"Where were we? Oh yes, in the room you are asked if you could do that. Live in a family of upset, unrest and unhappiness. You reply that you can do that, because you know who you are. You know you are that strong. Are you following me?"

"Yes... I like this."

"You are now born into this family and start your lessons. For years you have lived with the unpleasantness and now the real lessons start. Today, you are here because that part of you is waking up and wanting more, wanting to learn the why and how to fix this. The reason you are here on earth." Charlotte is nodding her head in agreement.

"So now it's time to separate yourself from Mom and Dad and start seeing them as a couple. They are like every couple; they chose each other for a reason. Maybe a choice made from a place of insecurity, unhappiness or fear. But all I want you to do is know that they are a couple and just like you with your boyfriend, they make mistakes and argue. If they have never stopped to look at the relationship, years of pain would only make it worse. Is this making sense?"

"Yes, it is, I never thought of my life in this way before and I definitely never thought about my parents like that!"

"I am going to have you do something for me. Close your eyes and take a breath, a deep breath. Now take another deep, deep breath. Just feel your body relax. Take a long slow deep breath and hold it. Now let go. Keep your eyes closed. Now I want you to see yourself in a room all by yourself. Can you do this?"

"Yes."

"Look around, there is a door way over there. Do you see it?"

"Yes."

"Go over to the door, put your hand on the knob, turn it and open the door. Walk through and look around. What do you see?"

"Hmm, I see a big tree, huge. A huge tree."

"Do you want to walk over to it?"

"Yes."

"Now I want you to do whatever you want and tell me what you are doing."

"I'm walking toward the tree, it's so big. I just want to sit under it. I feel like it's calming. I want to relax, just breathe. I'm just sitting. It feels good."

"Stay there as long as you like, let me know when you want to do something more."

Five minutes went by before Charlotte spoke again. "A bird sat on my leg! It's not scared of me at all. It's beautiful, bright red and looking right at me!"

"Just sit with it. Can you hear anything?"

"It's like he's trying to tell me something. I feel like he is with me, like an angel? Someone I know."

"That is good, keep connecting with him."

"I feel like he is watching over me."

"Do you want to ask him anything?"

"No, this feels strangely familiar. I just want to be here."

"Feel peaceful?"

"Yes." Another five minutes go by and Lily asks Charlotte how she is now. "I'm good. I'm not sure what happened but I feel I know who I am, I am strong. I know that I am the source of my happiness, even in this horrible life, but it all feels like it's not real."

"Before you open your eyes, I want you to picture your parents coming toward you. I want you to go to them and hug them. See that it is their pain and not your fault. See that this lesson was chosen by you before you were born and now you can move forward and learn from all the experience you have so far. They are stuck in their pain and suffering but you can move on now." Lily waited until Charlotte opened her eyes. "Now when you go home and see your parents the way you left them this morning, call on the image you saw, keep the understanding of what they are trying to learn. Can you do that?"

"I am going to try very hard."

"This is the important part, you must focus on you, your life, your goals, even when it gets bad. When you finish this school of lessons, you will be free. Free to leave, free to have a life of your own, a life you are in control of. Many people today are in pain. They need to find their own way out. All we can do is keep living, moving, healing, and holding the light so they may find their way out because we are not good when we are all in the darkness together. Understand?"

"Yes, I do. Can I come back? I may need a tune up to get to the next level or just to maintain how I feel now."

"Of course, you can. This is on- going but what you did today, just feeling the way you do is huge. Now you have something to call on when it gets hard, remember your imaging. I don't want to overwhelm you. Can you come back on Thursday morning and we can continue?" Charlotte agrees.

Her entire demeanor has changed. "Thank you, Lily, thank you so much." She gave Lily a big hug before leaving.

When she leaves, Lily sits behind her desk and just goes over the session in her mind. There is so much pain in the world. Lily sits and mediates to see the truth. She can only help the people that find her, she can not go into thoughts about the whole of life's truths, it's too overwhelming. She sits in gratitude that one person is on their way and that's all she can do. Lily knows that she grew up in a similar situation and it was her strength of imagination, positive thinking and just focusing on what she wanted and not what she didn't want in her life that made a world of difference. If Charlotte learns this then her siblings may have a chance, just by watching and seeing her attitude changes and her movement forward. Lily looked up at her new plaque and smiled.

Chapter Eleven

It was Tuesday night and Keith and Lily joined a large group in the bookstore for Greg's lecture on meditation. Lily watched Keith as Greg spoke and he seemed to be listening. She hoped this would help.

Afterwards Lily went to help Nicole with coffee and cakes and Keith walked into Greg's office. Greg looked up from his notes. "Well Keith, what did you think?"

"You know I don't believe in this stuff like you do. It's too hard in the environment I work in to keep it up and if I spoke like you, they would all think I'm crazy. I have trouble really seeing things from your perspective. I don't think sitting in the lotus position and being silent is going to help me."

"I have a few minutes, want to chat?" Greg pointed to the chair and was surprised when Keith sat down.

It was an hour later when Keith walked out of the office. Lily was standing near the door thanking people for coming. "Where have you been? You missed the coffee and cake."

"Never mind, I want to leave now." He seemed upset.

"What happened?"

"I get it now, okay! I finally get it! Now let's go home." He opened the door and walked out. Lily looked toward Glen's door, he was there with his hand raised. Lily looked puzzled.

"Take him home now Lily. He will be fine." Glen smiled.

In the car, Keith was silent. Lily didn't ask any questions, she would wait until he was ready but something had happened in Glen's office. When they reached the house, Keith looked at her. "I believe that there is something to all this spiritual stuff. Glen knew things I had never told anyone, even you. He freaked me out. Just let me absorb it, okay?"

"Of course, let's go and see the kids." Lily was overjoyed.

"Lily wait, I'm willing to try stuff at home but not at work."

A few days later, Keith woke up early and went into his study. He sat on the floor and closed his eyes. He felt foolish but he was determined to try. He sat for more than twenty minutes, silent and not thinking about anything. Finally, he opened his eyes and was surprised at how relaxed and calm he felt. *There might be something to all this spiritual mumbo jumbo after all. It can't hurt and I promised Glen I would at least try.*

He came into the kitchen where the family was gathered for breakfast. "Good morning, how is everyone today?" Lily looked over and smiled. Something was different about her husband.

Lily cleared the dishes before leaving for the office and thought about how Keith had changed in just a few days. She would stop in and see Glen later.

Glen was busy with clients when Lily arrived at the bookstore. She told Nicole about the change in Keith and her friend was thrilled. "Glen is an amazing healer, perhaps he made Keith realize there is more to life than appears on the surface. I am really happy for you Lily, I know you were worried."

"I am leaving Keith alone for now, I don't want to rush him. He will come to me when he is ready. Just like my clients, and speaking of clients, I better go to work. Have a wonderful day Nicole, and tell Glen I said thank you." Lily left the bookstore and headed up the stairs. She had a full day ahead of her.

Lily's first client arrives and Lily notices that she is walking strangely. Her entire body quite stiff.

"Good morning, Come in. Please take a seat."

"Good morning, my name is Lyla." The woman slowly lowers her body into the chair. "How are you today?"

"Not so good, that's why I'm here. I'm hoping to get some answers to my life and my ill health." Lily goes to the sideboard and prepares the tea. She chooses Ginger tea knowing it will help with any inflammation.

"Can you tell me a little of what's going on? Drink this, it might help."

"Well, my life is okay really." Lyla says defensively, "I just feel stuck in my job and want to leave but I can't for financial reasons." She takes a sip of tea and smiles at the surprising taste. She lets the heat of the ginger warm her entire body as she swallows. "I have been in this job for 20 years and hate it now. I don't like the people and it feels stale but I'm not sure what to do or where to go."

"How does it make you feel?"

"I feel depleted and frustrated."

"What do you need from me? I like to work off questions; it helps me. So what would you like to know?" Lily drinks her tea and watches the expression on Lyla's face. She is thinking.

"Well, I guess what do I do now?"

"Tell me specifics not generalities."

"I want to leave my job so, why can't I? I used to have courage and love life, but not so much anymore."

"The fear has you paralyzed. You still do have the courage but something made you think you can't move. Are you in a relationship?"

Lyla laughs. "I have a husband, however I feel that I need to work because I can't trust him to support the family. He doesn't work steady and just leaves jobs whenever he wants to. I can't so why should he be able to?"

"I can see that he is doing what you would like to do. Right?"

"Yes, but we have to support the family and I need to feel safe and secure."

"If you want to feel safe, why do you stay with him?"

"To feel safe!" Lyla realizes the irony in what she said and laughs. "I get it! I see what you are saying. I'm staying with him because I need to feel safe yet he doesn't make me feel safe. So, I work at a job I hate, to feel safe and neither are making me happy."

"That's right, was your family life stable?"

"Yes."

"This is where you have your wires crossed. Safety being with someone in your life is better than being alone in your mind. This is a conundrum . What you need to realize is that safety comes from within, not from other people. If we give them the power, they can abuse it. He is okay with what he is doing because you have made it safe for him to do so. Does this make sense?" Lyla nods. "What you need to understand is that you set this up and only you can turn this around. Have courage, pullback your energy, your support. Tell him you are quitting your job and looking for another. Then ask him for support, which means staying in his job until you find one you like. I know it sounds simple but it's all about you finding your inner courage and standing up for yourself."

"Wow, that sounds too simple. So most of what we do in our minds, is make it harder. And then it gives us an excuse not to do something about it. Right?"

"Yes, but it still feels hard to do that. You need to talk to him. Remember this is a scenario that you have made in your mind. Change how you see it going and it will change the outcome you now are seeing. Let's practice. Close your eyes, now just pull him into your sight, sit with him. Now tell him what you want to tell him, then wait to see if you hear anything." Lily stops and drinks her tea, leaving Lyla to finish her thoughts.

"I told him. I felt calm and he just smiled." Lyla was pleased with herself.

"Now this is what you do in real life. Focus on how this went until you speak to him."

Lily let this sink in before continuing. "Now for a job. I see you going north of where you are." Lyla seemed surprised.

"Funny you say that. I have applied to a couple of jobs, but I'm scared to change jobs and start all over. I know if I don't I will stay stuck and unhappy."

"So what is better? Unhappy in old place or unhappy in new fresh place?"

Lyla laughs, "Okay, I get it. Take a chance. Go for it!"

"That's right. Get an interview, get the job. You will have no problem if you follow through. Everything in you is asking for you to do this. I find most times when the pain of our lives gets so strong it's because we have ignored the signs and feelings to move forward. Now to address the stiffness you are experiencing."

"Yes, it is awful."

"When did it start?"

"We moved into an apartment one year ago. It was around that time, maybe eight months ago."

"I see chemicals. Are you around chemicals?"

"No, I don't think so. No more than anyone else."

"I definitely see chemicals as the cause of your stiffness. Somewhere around where you live, so I would ask to see what and where they spray. Request that they do not spray your apartment. I want you to come back in a week and tell me all of what you have done. Okay?"

"Okay, good. I'll see you in one week. I will take another morning off, I'm leaving anyway." Lyla smiled broadly, a new confidence shone in her eyes. Lily hugged her and walked her to the door.

After Lyla left, Lily felt good. She knew she had helped another client and it felt good.

As she watched Lyla go down the stairs, she turned toward her office. Standing in front of the door, she let her fingers brush the surface of the sign. Lily remembered the pimply faced boy at the sign shop and his frustration when she couldn't decide what she wanted on the sign. She could still see him as he drummed his fingers on the counter, waiting impatiently. And when she finally made her decision, he gave her a look of astonishment.

Her fingers rested on her name. "Lily Baxter." Directly beneath were the words, "Everyone Welcome." Lily did not like labels. Labels separated people in Lily's mind, and she was all about oneness. The pimply boy wanted her to add a line telling people her profession, but Lily knew that her clients didn't need labels. She was happy with the sign and she was very happy with her life.

The End

A Word from Janet Jordan Fitzgerald

I have always gone for help, whether it is spiritual, physical healing, or emotional healing, however I found that it became very expensive. Sometimes I just didn't go. The last thing I wanted was for this to happen to my clients. I knew how hard it was for me to continue, therefore I work on a sliding scale and help those who cannot afford this kind of work.

I had got a lot of criticism for not charging a lot more or "giving it away" but are we not here for one another? For everyone, not just those who can afford such help! Which I think is the way to healing. Some people are there to feed the belief that the more you charge, the better you are. Others are there to feed the belief that society does not have to dictate how good you are by how much you charge. The crazy thing is, we believe what the media tells us.

It's time to believe in who you are, but first you have to find yourself, because who we are was taught to us by life situations, people around us, by society. Question all of this and you start to see who YOU are. Peel the onion! The layers have to be peeled back. That's where I started.

By sharing our stories. we help others. I can't tell you how many times I have done a talk and people have come up to me and said, "It felt like you were talking just to me!" I believe that when I do a talk or retreat, everyone that comes, shares a common thread and at the end they really do see that. I love how it seems like magic, but really there is always a presence in the room. I like to call God. We are not so different, we just want to be heard, acknowledged in a world that teaches us to hide who we are, because it's not good enough. I say to hell with that...a change is coming!

https://www.youtube.com/channel/UCBtJuMjHw4z705gGZM3QCsQ

Watch Janet Jordan Fitzgerald on you tube.

CHAKRAS   OPENING   BALANCING

East meets west…chakra balancing….healing old wounds…..

CHAKRAS must flow like a river. They connect through the pools of energy. When Chakras are not flowing, they are blocked and can't flow. Open the Chakras and everything flows. Around 2500 B.C in India, the belief in chakras started. Chakra is a Sanskrit word meaning vortex, spinning wheel or circle.

Chakras and are circles of energy which balance, store and distribute the energies of life all through our physical body and are the major centers of spiritual power in the human body. Often said to act through the subtle body, which is the non- physical body or our soul or spirit, which overlays our physical body.

Chakras are circles of energy, flowing all the way through our body that assist in the running of our body, mind and soul. If a chakra is not performing correctly, physical health, mental health and our spiritual selves could suffer. The chakras start at the base of the spine and move upwards to the last one at the crown of the head.

1st) ROOT**TAILBONE***EARTH***SURVIVAL***

The Root Chakra can be blocked by fear. Relationships in our early life often affect this Chakra. This Chakra is often attached to social attitudes, religion or family. How do you see yourself? Surrender the fear to open.

2nd) SACRAL**PUBIC BONE***WATER***PLEASURE***

The Sacral Chakra can be blocked by guilt. It is often attached to survival, security and money. It is the source of inspiration and creativity. What do you feel guilty about? Accept and release the blame and the guilt. Forgive yourself.

3rd) SOLAR PLEXUS**ABOVE BELLYBUTTON***FIRE**
MONITORS ENERGY*** WILLPOWER***

The Solar Plexus Chakra is blocked by shame. It is attached to self esteem, intimacy and fear. What are your biggest disappointments in yourself? Do not deny this part of your life!

4th) HEART***LOVE***COMPASSION

The Heart Chakra is blocked by grief. It is attached to lack of harmony or a broken heart. Take a look at all of your grief. See your grief and accept it. Love is energy

5TH) THROAT***SOUND***TRUTH***

The throat Chakra is blocked by lies. It is attached to expressing yourself, communication, your truth. Who are you really? We cannot lie about our own nature. Do not lie to yourself.

6TH) THIRD EYE***LIGHT ***CENTER OF FORHEAD***

The third eye Chakra is blocked by illusion and separation. We see ourselves as divided, separate from others. We are all one, everyone is connected.

7TH) CROWN**** TOP OF HEAD*** COSMIC ENERGY…

The crown Chakra is blocked by attachments. It is attached to Grace, stored prayers and true connection to spirit. Who or what are your attachments? Let go of all things and people you are attached to, this does not mean you do not love them, quite the contrary. It does not mean the people or things disappear. It is replacing attachment for unconditional love. Many are unable to release and unblock this Chakra.

Usually a typical person swings psychologically between compulsion for gratification ad escaping the bitterness of life, which is related to an imbalanced and underdeveloped work of the three lowest chakras. The life most people live is fighting for survival, making money, sexual lust, obsessed by attachment to food, striving for self-esteem by controlling others, creating a fake reality with 'I', 'Me' and 'Mine' being the center. But nothing physical really lasts. All material victories and failures are gone in time, sooner or later.

Chakras can also be linked to illness in that part of the body. Eastern medicine works on all levels of the body, mind spirit.

When one of the Chakras is out, you are out of balance. Past Pain, Trauma, being unloved, abandoned, and many more things can contribute to states of illness of mind, body, spirit.

I would highly recommend getting a 'clearing' if one or more of your Chakras are blocked. To truly understand our Chakras, please read one of the many books focusing solely on Chakras. There are also websites and Youtube videos pertaining to Chakras.

MEDITATION

Meditation is the method of sitting or lying quietly and letting your thoughts disappear. To focus and quiet your mind is the goal of meditation, eventually reaching a higher level of awareness and inner calm. You can meditate anywhere and at any time, allowing yourself to access a sense of tranquility and peace no matter what's going on around you. This short article will introduce you to the basics of meditation. Whether you just need to relax or want to begin your journey on the path of enlightenment and bliss, meditation will improve your health and your well- being.

To begin, sit or lay in a quiet place where you will not be disturbed. Relax your body and close your eyes. Now take a MEDITATION breath and hold, BREATHE and hold. Now just breathe normally but focus on your breath. Don't force it or change it, just focus on it.

.How do you feel? Experience how you feel. Hold and release your breath. It is the easiest and most effective tool to learning to meditate, as your mind is busy focusing on your breath, it is not buzzing with other thoughts. Do this three or four times. You will feel the effect of the mind quieting. You may want to do it for a few minutes or much longer.

MEDITATION.....HOW TO VISUALIZE.....

In your mind, imagine a room. You pick the room but make it come alive in your mind. Now spend time in this room, touch the furniture, smell the air, experience the feeling of the room.

MEDITATION...FEELINGS.....AWARNESS....

Take a tour through your body. Begin at your toes and work upwards slowly. What do you feel? Just put your attention on parts of your body be aware of how that part of your body feels. Practice this and soon you will know how each part and organ feels. (if you have a problem area focus on it longer and see how it feels after giving it attention)

     MEDITATION……HOLD FOCUS….

     Picture what you want in your mind. It can be anything. Just keep bringing your focus back to what you want. It is like daydreaming or fantasizing. You are making it real in your mind. Remember "As within so without" Now notice the sounds around you but don't try to block them out. Put it all together and do a meditation.

     There is no wrong way to meditate the simple act that you are sitting down with intention and breathing. Just keep trying. The only intention you need is to sit, do nothing and allow your mind and body to relax. Don't fight it, just concentrate on your breath. Your body knows what to do.

EMPATHY

Empaths are in-tune with or resonate with others, voluntarily or involuntarily. They have the ability to read and understand people.

Empaths are able to scan the psyche for thoughts and feelings and also for past, present, and future life occurrences. Most empaths will admit they are unaware of how this actually works, and have simply accepted that they were sensitive to others.

Empaths can relate to a person by sensing true feelings hidden below the surface. Once the empath senses the truth, he or she will act compassionately to help that person express their true feelings. This makes them feel at ease and not desperately alone.

An empath can feel the emotions of people and things at a distance. They are highly sensitive. Generally, most empaths grow up with these tendencies and do not learn to recognize them until later in life. Empathy can vary in level of strength and starts with the individual's awareness of self, and their understanding of the powers of empathy.

Empathy is inherent in our DNA and therefore genetic. Empaths observe what another is saying, feeling and thinking, and by doing this they come to understand another. Empaths are very proficient at reading another person's body language.

Studies of Empaths show some results. Because we know everything has an energetic vibration or frequency, we now understand that an empath is able to sense these vibrations and recognize the subtle changes.

Empaths are the excellent listeners. They are often problem solvers, thinkers, and scholars. An empath always feels that where a problem exists, so too does the answer There are many books, websites and reference sources for Empaths and Empathy.

Recommended Reading List

You can heal your life	Louise Hay
Emotional Awareness	Gary Zukav
The Road less traveled	Dr M Scott Peck
The Third Eye	T. Lobsang Rampa
Coming Home	John Bradshaw
Living from the Heart	Nirmala
Nothing Personal	Nirmala
That is That	Nirmala

There are many books on the subjects covered here, I encourage you to seek the information you need and don't be afraid to ask for help. Thank you for taking the time to read Lily, A Modern Day Healer and I hope you enjoyed it.

Made in the USA
Middletown, DE
25 November 2017